COSTA BLANCA

T0001767

Travel with Marco Polo Insider Tips

MARCO POLO TOP HIGHLIGHTS

PEÑÍSCOLA OLD TOWN ⭐1
Narrow streets, cosy bars and steep ascents to the castle: Peñíscola is one of the Costa Blanca's most beautiful towns.
📷 *Tip: Check out the view of the old town from both the beach and the castle.*

➤ p. 44, Costa del Azahar

SERRA D'IRTA NATURE RESERVE ⭐2
Dense pine forests, lonely paths and breathtaking views of the mountains and the sea: a dream for hikers.

➤ p. 48, Costa del Azahar

LLOTJA DE LA SEDA ⭐3
The magnificent old Silk Exchange in València is a UNESCO World Heritage Site.

➤ p. 62, València

CIUTAT DE LES ARTS I LES CIÈNCIES ⭐4
València's "City of Arts and Sciences" is a masterpiece of modern architecture.
📷 *Tip: Go early in the morning and late in the afternoon, when the buildings are reflected in the water.*

➤ p. 63, València

LAS FALLAS ⭐5
During València's largest folk festival in March, the city and other towns are first abuzz, then ablaze.
📷 *Tip: For the best pictures of the papier-mâché figures, aim for the blue hour shortly after sunset.*

➤ p. 64, València, p.123, Festivals & events

L'ALBUFERA ⭐ 6

Herons, ducks, reed-covered canals: this nature reserve near València is one of the most species-rich biotopes in the country (photo).

➤ p. 68, València

BENIDORM'S BEACHES ⭐ 7

The Levante and Poniente beaches are top-notch sandy strands.

📷 *Tip: Head to the Balcón del Mediterráneo in the old town for the best view of both beaches.*

➤ p. 83, Costa Blanca

CARTAGENA ⭐ 9

A Roman theatre, a Punic city wall and a beautiful natural harbour – Cartagena is a real gem.

📷 *Tip: The castle hill in the old town offers views in all directions.*

➤ p. 105, Costa Cálida/Mar Menor

GUADALEST ⭐ 8

Alleyways afford glimpses of the mountains and valleys that surround this picturesque hilltop village.

➤ p. 87, Costa Blanca

ÁGUILAS'S BEACHES ⭐ 10

Sandy or rocky, busy or secluded? Discover your dream cove in southern Murcia.

➤ p. 110, Costa Cálida/Mar Menor

CONTENTS

■ CONTENTS ■

⏱	Plan your visit	🍴	Eating/drinking	🌂	Rainy day activities
€-€€€	Price categories	🛍	Shopping	🦇	Budget activities
(*)	Premium-rate phone number	🍸	Nightlife	🎭	Family activities
		🏖	Best beaches	🚩	Classic experiences

(🗺 A2) Removable pull-out map
(0) Address located off the pull-out map

Belltower and gateway at Guadalest

BEST OF THE COSTA BLANCA

The Penyal d'Ilfac is a distinctive feature of the coast near Calp

BEST WHEN IT RAINS

ACTIVITIES TO BRIGHTEN YOUR DAY

LIQUEUR TASTING

Descend into a world of spirits in the *Bodegas Carmelitano* in Benicàssim. The tour of the traditional cellars also includes a tasting session.

➤ p. 50, Costa del Azahar

ART & SCIENCE

You'll find plenty to do on a rainy day at the *Ciutat de les Arts i les Ciències*. The interactive Science Museum and the *Hemisfèric*, with its IMAX screenings, are also impressive examples of modern architecture.

➤ p. 63, València

TEMPLE OF THE ARTS

The *Museu de Belles Arts* in València is Spain's second-largest art gallery. It is a temple of the arts, with works by Spanish masters from the 15th to 19th centuries, including Goya, Sorolla and Velázquez (photo).

➤ p. 64, València

PALACE OF REFUGE

From the 14th century, the enormous *Palau Ducal dels Borja* was the residence of the royal dukes of Gandia, including the power-hungry Borgia dynasty from 1485. What few know, however, is that the Borgias even had a pope within their ranks.

➤ p. 76, Costa Blanca

AT HOME WITH THE ROMANS

The *Museu del Teatro Romano* in Cartagena brings Ancient Rome to life in a unique museum. Exhibits, including jewellery, busts and accessories are integrated into the cityscape by incorporating the 2,000-year-old remains of the city wall.

➤ p. 105, Costa Cálida

![BEST 🐷 ON A BUDGET](FOR SMALLER WALLETS)

THE JOYS OF THE SADDLE

How about borrowing a *bicycle free of charge*? This is possible in Benicàssim on the Costa del Azahar, where the town rents out bicycles for a 50-euro deposit and an ID card.

➤ p. 51, Costa del Azahar

ART FOR FREE

Admission to the *Museu Belles Arts (Museum of Fine Arts)* in Castelló de la Plana is free of charge. The main focus are works by Francisco de Osona, Juan de Juanes and Juan Ribalta, with oil paintings by Francisco de Zurbarán. Ceramics and archaeological finds complete the museum's collection.

➤ p. 54, Costa del Azahar

JAZZ FOR FREE

Miles Davis would have been in heaven: every August, the small mountain village of Polop is transformed into a stage for the free *Jazzpolop* festival. Artists come together from Spain and all over the world with music played late into the night.

➤ p. 83, Costa Blanca

MONUMENTAL DUO

There are two interesting architectural sights to visit in Novelda, and you do not have to pay for either of them: the small castle *La Mola* and the monastery of *Santa María Magdalena*, with its elaborate decoration influenced by the Catalan form of art nouveau known as *Modernisme*.

➤ p. 96, Costa Blanca

TREASURES FROM THE SEA

Greek amphorae, Carthaginian coins, Roman plates: if you want to see precious and peculiar things that have ended up on the ocean floor over the centuries, you should visit the *Museo Nacional de Arqueología Subacuática* in Cartagena (photo); there is no admission fee on weekends.

➤ p. 106, Costa Cálida/Mar Menor

BEST WITH CHILDREN

FUN FOR YOUNG & OLD

PARROT WATCHING

The vibrant parrot garden (*Jardín del Papagayo*) near Peñíscola includes walk-in aviaries with 500 colourful birds fluttering around. What is more, there are flight shows, a butterfly house and a kangaroo zone.

➤ p. 46, Costa del Azahar

UNDERWORLD ADVENTURES

What an incredible experience! Hop on a boat in the *Coves de Sant Josep* near Vall d'Uixó and explore the underground world of caves, rivers and lakes. Highlights include the "Cathedral" and the "Hall of Bats".

➤ p. 55, Costa del Azahar

ELEPHANTS, RHINOS & FRIENDS

At *Terra Natura* near Benidorm, kids get the chance to get up close and personal with big animals, including elephants, rhinos and big cats.

➤ p. 83, Costa Blanca

SWIM WITH SEA LIONS

All sorts of creatures swim, jump and fly at the *Mundomar* zoo near Benidorm, including dolphins, sea lions (which you can swim with), lemurs, penguins, parrots and flamingos.

➤ p. 84, Costa Blanca

SAFARI ON FOOT

Safari on foot? Yes, it really is a thing! At *Río Safari Elche*, you can spot parrots, lemurs, giraffes and elephants. There's even a safari ferry, crocodile farm and "reptile cave".

➤ p. 94, Costa Blanca

SHOCK & AWE

There are water slides for all at *Aquópolis Torrevieja*! On the "Kamikaze" slide you zoom into the refreshing water at a breathtaking pace, while "Speed" and "Boomerang" are also guaranteed to increase your pulse rate whatever your age (photo).

➤ p. 97, Costa Blanca

BEST 🏳

CLASSIC EXPERIENCES

ONLY ON THE COSTA BLANCA

DECORATIVE, HEALTHY & TASTY

Delicious oranges ripen on trees in countless plantations in this region, and the northern part of the coast, the Costa del Azahar ("Orange Blossom Coast") is even named after the white flowers. You can stock up on fresh oranges at *Frutas Piñana* in Peñíscola.
➤ p. 47, Costa del Azahar

BLAZING FIESTA FUN

Fireworks and bangers are always part of *Las Fallas*, one of the region's most important annual *fiestas*. Artists give free rein to their wit and imagination in their oversized papier-mâché figures, which are displayed on the streets until the "Night of Fire", when everything goes up in flames.
➤ p. 64, València, p. 123 Festivals & events

FAMOUS RICE DISH

The entire region around València is regarded as the home of *paella* (photo). Restaurants compete to serve the best. *Casa Carmela*, right on La Malva-Rosa beach, is known for dishing up the very best in the business.
➤ p. 66, València

SPAIN'S MANHATTAN?

Pretty crass, yet somehow with its own charm, Benidorm – widely regarded as the cradle of mass tourism in Spain – has a skyline that includes more than 300 high-rises. Luckily it also boasts two dreamy stretches of sand: the *Platja de Llevant* and *Platja de Ponent*.
➤ p. 83, Costa Blanca

COMMANDING CASTLES

Numerous watchtowers and castles, many dating back to the Moors, can be seen along the coast. In the Middle Ages, many fell to the Christians who adapted them for their purposes. The impressive *Castell de Santa Bárbara*, dominates the skyline over Alicante.
➤ p. 89, Costa Blanca

GET TO KNOW THE COSTA BLANCA

Sun-ripened oranges are one of the region's most important exports

DISCOVER THE COSTA BLANCA

A platform in Benidorm provides an uninterrupted view of the sea

Pure, golden happiness on a plate – in this case, a plain white porcelain plate, the delicacy barely the size of the palm of your hand. "Deep-fried cod," announces Goi Cortázar, her eyes lighting up as she walks over to the table. And rightly so! What she serves up really is the stuff of dreams: the breadcrumb coating, fried in oil, mingles with the tender flesh of the cod to create the most exquisite taste sensation.

A REGION REDEFINED

Moments later, Cortázar dishes out yet more delicacies: fried artichoke hearts, green asparagus, paper-thin pork tenderloin and, of course, the feted *pimientos de Padrón*, mini peppers dipped in coarse salt. In fact, it would be easy to walk right past the *Cervecería Xeito de Goi* on Altea's waterside promenade, but what

3rd century BC–4th century AD Roman rule	711 Moors invade the Iberian Peninsula, leading to a flowering of Islamic culture	1492 End of the Reconquista, in which the territories occupied by the Moors are taken by Christian forces	1808–14 French invasion led by Napoleon Bonaparte	1936–39 Spanish Civil War, followed by dictatorship under Franco	1960s Economic boom, introduction of mass tourism

a shame that would be! The restaurant is one of the very best along the entire coast, the perfect symbol of a region in the process of regeneration. Long dubbed the birthplace of mass tourism, Spain's southeastern coast is gradually becoming something altogether more creative. Despite the Covid-19 pandemic, which negatively impacted many businesses, a whole host of new tapas bars, cute boutique hotels and independent shops are springing up on every corner.

Bordered by the Costa Brava in the north and Andalusia in the south, the region is split into three sections: the Costa del Azahar (the "orange blossom coast"), including Peñíscola and Benicàssim; the Costa Blanca (the "white coast"), with Altea, Benidorm and Calp; and the Costa Cálida (the "hot coast") around La Manga and the Mar Menor in the south. As if that weren't enough, right at the heart lies València, Spain's third-largest city and an urban island in a holiday paradise, complete with fantastic architecture and fascinating museums.

300 DAYS OF SUNSHINE

Long before today's holidaymakers, the Phoenicians, the Iberians, the Romans and later the Moors all enjoyed what this coastline has to offer. But why? Well, the climate for one: 300 fine days per year make this region the sunniest location in Europe. Plus, many of the cultural treasures left behind by early settlers can still be seen today. If you fancy something Phoenician, head to the settlement of La Fonteta near Alicante, or try the famous bust of Dama de Elx for a taste of the Iberians

1975
End of Franco's military dictatorship; Juan Carlos named King

1978
The new constitution comes into force and Spain becomes a democracy

1986
Spain becomes the 11th member of the EU

2010
Spain wins the football World Cup

2014
After years of recession, Spain begins to regain economic stability

2020-21
The Covid-19 pandemic hits Spain and impacts tourism

(although the original is safely in the National Museum in Madrid). For something Roman, there are a range of buildings in Sagunt and Cartagena, while traces of the Moors remain in countless words and place names, dozens of fortresses and, of course, the *acequia* irrigation system still used today. These days, however, it is primarily tourists who are keen to take advantage of Spain's southeast coast. The '60s and '70s saw former fishing villages like Benidorm, Calp and La Manga transform into veritable cities of hotels. Alongside the package holidaymakers, an army of emigrés and sun-seekers from Britain and other countries in northern and central Europe make this spot their home for at least a few months a year.

BLOOMING MARVELLOUS

While most visitors may be familiar with this coast's high-rise blocks, holiday homes and long beaches, they soon discover that Spain's eastern coast has far more to offer. The Sant Antoni and Nao capes jut out spectacularly into the Mediterranean between Dénia and Calp; the beautiful coastal mountain ranges, such as El Montgó near Dénia and Serra d'Irta near Peñíscola, attract hikers, as does the Sierra Helada near Albir. There are equally impressive landscapes to be discovered in the hinterland. Just a few kilometres inland from Benidorm, the air is full of the aroma of pine trees and herbs, while oranges and lemons, olives, almonds, medlars and figs all flourish under the southern sun. The white facades of the houses in many villages are made more dazzling by the hibiscus and bougainvillea blossoms; the countryside is carpeted with ice plants *(delosperma)*, agaves and prickly pear cactuses.

NON-STOP PARTIES

The region's colourful past has left it with a thriving cultural legacy, which is reflected in its *fiestas*. Alongside the usual celebrations for each local saint, many towns recreate the bombastic battles between the Moors and the Christians *(Moros y Cristianos)*. The world-famous *Las Fallas* celebration in València is a sort of mass-scale Guy Fawkes night where politicians and public figures are cruelly caricatured as ginormous papier-mâché effigies (and later burned!). Plus, there are a whole host of other more unusual celebrations, like the tomato battle in Buñol near València or the flour fight in Ibi near Alicante.

In culinary terms, one dish, in particular, has made the region famous: *paella valenciana*. This traditional dish is the crowning glory of Valencian cuisine, and no event, fiesta or family celebration is complete without that famous pan of rice. It may not be on Goi Cortázar's menu, but you can still enjoy the freshest produce here, from the sea, the mountains and the fields. For the final time this evening, Cortázar ambles out onto the terrace holding a portion of *setas al roquefort*, mushrooms bathed in Roquefort sauce, which she sets down on the table. "I can't eat any more," I say to her. "But it's a house speciality! It would be rude not to try it," jokes Cortázar. "I'll do my best," I think, before my tastebuds are flooded with delicious flavours all over again.

AT A GLANCE

6,500,000
Population (regions of València and Murcia combined)

Scotland: 5,460,000

770km
coastline (from Vinaròs in the north to Aguilas in the south)
England's southwest coast (from Minehead to Poole): 1,014km

8.3
Average sunshine hours per day in Alicante

Eastbourne: 4.8

HIGHEST MOUNTAIN: PICO DEL OBISPO (MURCIA)

2,014m
Ben Nevis: 1,345m

HOTTEST MONTH

AUGUST
31°C
MEASURED IN ALICANTE

UNESCO WORLD HERITAGE SITES:

12
IN THE REGIONS OF VALÈNCIA AND MURCIA
LONDON: 4

THE WORLD'S LARGEST PAELLA

The pan used to cook the paella was a whopping 20m in diameter and fed 100,000 in València on 8 March 1992

VALÈNCIA
Biggest city, with a population of 795,000

18.5km
Length of La Manga coastal strip

OVER 300 HIGH-RISE BUILDINGS IN BENIDORM

UNDERSTAND THE COSTA BLANCA

REGIONAL DIVERSITY

Regional differences are a source of both celebration and ridicule in Spain – just as they are in the UK. Inhabitants of different regions like to joke about their compatriots in other parts of the country. The Catalans in the northeast, for example, are characterised as thrifty, stubborn and punctual, while the Galicians and Basques on the north coast have a reputation for grumpiness and secrecy. Those who live on the southeast coast, however, seem to fit the Spanish stereotype – it might just be a result of more than 300 days of sunshine a year, mild winters and the eternal turquoise of the Mediterranean, but people here are relaxed, friendly and open.

Let's get up to speed with a few key facts. With just under 47 million inhabitants, Spain is the fifth-largest market economy in Europe. The *Comunitat Valenciana* and the *Región de Murcia* are two of the autonomous regions that make up Spain and can be compared with states in the USA. Since the death of the dictator Franco in 1975, Spain has undergone a complete overhaul, including adopting a democratic constitution in 1978. Today, King Felipe VI is the country's head of state. Spain was hit hard by the economic crisis in 2008; in the years that followed, hundreds of thousands of Spaniards took to the streets to demonstrate against austerity, unemployment and corruption. In time, this civic movement would become known as the *Movimiento 15 de Mayo* (15 May movement) and can take credit for the emergence of new political parties that would go on to take power at a regional level. Even in holiday regions on the coast, local and national politics, coupled with the Catalan dream of independence, can lead to some heated discussions.

ONE COAST, TWO LANGUAGES

1982 was a historic year for many Valencians. That was the year Article 7.2 of the Statute of the Autonomous Community of València recognised Valencian as the region's official language alongside Spanish. It's worth noting that what we call Spanish is actually Castilian (*castellano*), while Valencian is known as *valencià (valenciano)*. Linguistically, *valencià* is a Catalan dialect, making Catalonia a far closer neighbour for *Valencianos* than the central bureaucratic power base in Madrid. But don't make the mistake of telling a Valencian native they speak *català*. While the two languages are 95 per cent identical, that five per cent makes all the difference!

The region's diglossia can result in some confusion for tourists. Imagine you are in the centre of a town or village looking for a street on the map in your hand. The names on the map are in Spanish but those on the house walls are in Valencian – not at all unusual in this mixed-language region! In

Valencian "street" is *carrer*; in Spanish, *calle*. There are also different words for "avenue" (Valencian *avinguda*; Spanish *avenida*) and "square" (*plaça/plaza*). In this guide, we use the standard Spanish abbreviations: *C/* for *Carrer/Calle*, *Av.* for *Avinguda/Avenida*, *Pl.* for *Plaça/plaza* and *s/n* for *sin número*, "without a house number".

SPORTING THRILLS

Whatever the language, the best way to befriend a Spaniard is to turn the conversation to football. The sport is deeply rooted in Spanish culture. The national team won the European Championship in 2008 and 2012 and won the World Cup in 2010, while Spanish clubs Real Madrid, Atlético de Madrid and F.C. Barcelona are among the most successful teams in European club football. The Costa Blanca region is currently well-represented in Spain's *Primera División* with three teams: F.C. València, Villarreal CF and Elche CF.

Although interest is waning among younger people, ⚑ bullfights *(corridas de toros)* remain firmly established in Spain's cultural identity. Every self-respecting town has a bullring *(plaza de toros)*, and although animal rights activists regularly hold demonstrations against the practice, bullfights still attract spectators in their thousands. A less bloodthirsty (but still not animal-friendly) variation are the races against bulls and cows that take place mainly in the countryside. At the *Bous al Carrer*, anyone with the "courage" to risk life and limb can run around in front of the animals. A more unusual iteration is the *Bous al Mar* in Denia (July), where the bull ends up in the harbour.

Valencian street sign marking "Museum Street"

Elaborate papier-mâché figures all go up in smoke during *Las Fallas*

HEROES, SAINTS & FIESTAS

You could easily fill an entire travel guide with the region's manifold festivals. The *Comunitat Valenciana* loves a *fiesta* – and the associated firecrackers, bangers and fireworks (which no *fiesta* is complete without). Highlights are *Las Fallas* in València in March and the *Hogueras de San Juan* near Alicante in June. Both *fiestas* see incredible papier-mâché figures, often several stories high, torched on 19 March and 23 June respectively. For those sensitive to noise, it's probably better to give the *mascletàs*, as the pyrotechnics are called, a wide berth. The fireworks only last five to eight minutes, but they are usually set alight with firecrackers and bangers that resemble hand grenades in the volume of noise they generate.

Another cracking feature of the regional calendar are the bombastic battles between the *Moros y Cristianos* ("Moors and Christians"), which are celebrated along the entire coastline with as much historic gun smoke as you could ever wish for. One of the most beautiful is the *fiesta* in La Vila Joiosa (July), where the "Moors" attack the city from the sea.

INSIDER TIP
Naval battl par excellence

The region also hosts many other curious festivities, such as the flour battle in Ibi near Alicante (December) or the tomato battle in Bunyol near València (August). This *tomatina* sees people hurl overripe tomatoes at one another for an hour. Registration is now mandatory in light of the growing influx of visitors from all over the world in recent years (*latomatina info*).

ART & LITERATURE

Francisco Ribalta (1565–1628) and his son, Juan Ribalta (1596–1628), who – curiously enough – both died in the same year, are considered masters of Valencian Baroque painting. The painter Antonio Fillol Granell (1870–1930), who devoted himself to social realism, also originated from València, as did the sculptor Mariano Benlliure (1862–1947) and the painter Joaquín Sorolla (1863–1923), a renowned proponent of Impressionism. Among other subjects, Sorolla's works depict the beach and the fishing villages along the coast of the Levante. The poet Vicente Blasco Ibáñez (1867–1928) was one of Sorolla's contemporaries; it is possible to visit Ibáñez's house – now a museum – in València. Several of his books – including *The Cabin, The Four Horsemen of the Apocalypse* and *Blood and Sand* – have been translated into English.

MODERN ARCHITECTURE

Spaniards love good design and architecture. You are likely to be familiar with the work of Antoni Gaudí and *Modernisme*, the Spanish version of Art Nouveau, but there are plenty of other styles and architects to admire. In València – check out the central market hall as well as the northern train station; the Casa Carbonell on the main promenade in Alicante and the Casa del Pavo in the heart of the small town of Alcoi also testify to architectural greatness. València is proud of being home to one of the major flagships of modern architecture in Spain: the City of Arts and Sciences *(Ciutat de*

TRUE OR FALSE?

THERE'S NEVER ENOUGH PAELLA

Every self-respecting *Valenciano* loves nothing more than paella. Each Sunday, the family chef brings out the giant paella pan, often as big as a wagon wheel, and fills it up with rice and other ingredients, much to everyone's satisfaction. Once it's ready, everyone tucks right into the pan – as it always has been! According to the *Guinness Book of Records*, the largest-ever paella was dished up in València in 1992 , with 5,000kg of rice serving 100,000 people. The pan itself was 20m in diameter.

CATALAN, RIGHT?

Valencianos speak a dialect of Catalan, and the *Comunitat Valenciana* borders Catalonia. So, *Valencianos* are Catalan, right? Well, watch out, because you won't be popular if you go round saying that on the Río Turia, that's for sure. *Valencianos* are no less proud of their identity than their neighbours to the north, even if they don't hold the same separatist ambitions. *Valencià* is taught alongside Spanish in schools, and place-name signs are often in the local language.

les Arts i les Ciènces) covers an area of 86 acres out of town. The site became a vast playground for star architect Santiago Calatrava, who was given free rein to express himself without a thought to anything as inconvenient as cost! Who thinks of bankruptcy anyway when faced with the *Palau des Arts Reina Sofía* opera house or the *Museu de les Ciències Príncipe Felipe*?

SOUNDS LIKE ARABIC

Think you don't know a word of Arabic? Think again – what about names like Altea, Alicante or Benidorm? This is because the Moors were a constant presence in Spain for around 780 years, from AD 711 to 1492. For these seven centuries, medicine, astrology and water management flourished, with the old Moorish water channels *(acequias)* still in use today. In fact, the legacy of the Moors is clear in many places to this day, their heritage even leaving its mark on the language and place names. Beni, for example, means something along the lines of "father of…"; countless places bear this prefix today: Benicarló, Benicàssim, Benidorm, Benimantell, Benifató, Beniardà. Words beginning with "al" stem from Arabic, too: not just places like Algemesí and Alhama de Murcia, but also nouns like pillow *(almohada)*, dressing gown *(albornoz)* and carpet *(alfombra)*. Want a fun game for your little ones? Grab the folding map in this book and hunt for as many towns as possible beginning with "Beni"!

CRISES & CORRUPTION

Two crises have hit Spain, and particularly the Mediterranean coast with its reliance on tourism, in recent years: the financial crisis in the years after 2008 and the Covid-19 pandemic of 2020/21. Unemployment rose to 20 per cent among all age groups during the economic crash, hitting 50 per cent among young people. Meanwhile, the long-term financial impact of the pandemic, which caused many businesses to close – some for good – is still unclear.

But there are other factors that shouldn't be swept under the carpet. This region has suffered from architectural megalomania, corruption and political profligacy. There are building projects that were never completed, now reduced to crumbling plaster and concrete skeletons. Certainly, few other places in Spain have seen as much construction and decay as Spain's southeast coast, and València ranks among the country's most indebted cities. For years, it has been striving to compete with Madrid and Barcelona: to boast a more beautiful opera house than Madrid and a bigger port than Barcelona. But this ambition has cost the city a lot of money – money that is now missing from València's coffers.

There's also the fact that, since the start of the tourism boom back in the 1960s, many people in the region have given up farming in favour of *ladrillo*, literally "brick". In other words, they have invested in real estate. Sadly, this decision has often left locals vulnerable to recent economic shocks.

València's Palau de les Arts embodies the architectural flair of its creator, Santiago Calatrava

EATING
SHOPPING
SPORT

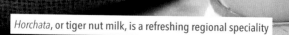
Horchata, or tiger nut milk, is a refreshing regional speciality

EATING & DRINKING

From paella to almond milk, a surprisingly meagre breakfast, tapas in between meals and the art of dining for hours on end: Spain's southeast coast has a whole host of culinary surprises in store.

START THE DAY... RIGHT?

The Spanish don't tend to skimp when it comes to creature comforts. All the more surprising therefore that breakfast *(desayuno)* is kept short and sweet for most people: a quick sip of coffee *(cortado* or *café con leche)*, a croissant, a *churro* – a stick-shaped doughnut coated in sugar – or white toast with olive oil, grated tomato and salt. And that's pretty much it. Spaniards are much more interested in lunch *(almuerzo)*, served from 2pm onwards. Many bars and restaurants serve mixed platters *(platos combinados)* and tapas. Favourites include Serrano ham *(jamón serrano)*, meatballs *(albóndigas)* and the ⚑ Spanish national dish *tortilla española*, a kind of potato omelette. Most Spaniards, however, prefer to tuck into a full multi-course lunch. The traditional three-course daily menus *(menú del día)* are a common sight on weekdays in particular and are a solid choice for lunch. Plus, the whole thing – including a drink and coffee – is usually no more than 6 to 8 euros.

C FOR CENA

Just like lunch, dinner *(cena)* starts later here too. In days gone by, you'd have been hard-pressed to find a cook willing to enter their kitchen before 8.30pm. In the resorts on the coast, however, local restaurant owners have adapted to the habits of their foreign guests and tend to offer an earlier dinner option. Dinner typically begins with a few small starters shared by the table: *pan i aioli*, white bread with

Tapas: Serrano ham with goat's cheese (left); *gambas al ajillo* (right)

garlic mayonnaise, as well as olives or a salad are all popular options. Next comes the main course, which is usually meat or fish with rice or vegetables. A good number of restaurants also serve vegetarian dishes on request – or at least a platter of fresh vegetables.

MEAT & FISH
For the best fish, head to the eateries near the fishing ports or the local *lonja*, where the catch-of-the-day is auctioned off. These fish auction halls can be found all along the coast, even in the smaller towns. Peñiscola, València, Calp, La Vila Joiosa and Alicante all have especially lovely halls. Popular fish and seafood include sea bass (*lubina*), monkfish (*rape*), sole (*lenguado*), tuna (*atún*), squid (*calamar*), octopus (*pulpo*), baby squid (*chipirones*), mussels (*mejillones*), scampi (*cigalas*), razor clams (*navajas*), prawns (*gambas*) and langoustine

(*langostinos*). Popular meat dishes include *chorizo*, the hearty pork sausage flavoured with garlic and paprika, beef tenderloin (*solomillo de ternera*) and lamb chops (*chuletas de cordero*).

SAVE THE SWEET TILL LAST
Spaniards like sweet things. The high sugar content of some of the desserts and cakes might seem too much for visitors from other parts of Europe, but they are delicious. A must-try classic is *flan casero*, a homemade custard pudding made from eggs and sugar. Alicante and, above all, Xixona are the home of *turrones*, traditional nut or almond honey bars, which can be anything from smooth and creamy to nutty and hard. The oranges (*naranjas*) grown on the plantations in the region are used to produce juice or sold to be eaten. Watermelon (*sandía*) and honeydew melon (*melón*) are also great for dessert.

Gratin-topped fish with fresh asparagus

SUNDAYS ARE FOR PAELLA

These days you can find the classic Valencian dish in almost any restaurant on the coast on any day of the week. For Spaniards, however, the real day for paella is Sunday, when families cook up enough paella to serve a small army in their trusty 🚩 giant rice pans. Meat, fish, seafood or just plain vegetables – the options are never-ending, although the traditional ingredients for the *paella valenciana* are chicken, rabbit and vegetables. Tired of paella? Try *fideuá*. Legend has it a couple of fishermen from Gandia invented the dish around 100 years ago when they ran out of rice and in their hunger substituted pasta for the base. One final note of caution: the Sunday paella ceremony can last for hours on end!

IN YOUR GLASS

The wine-growing areas in València and Alicante have a protected designation of origin (*Denominación de Origen*, or DO for short). A little further inland, the Utiel-Requena, Yecla and Jumilla areas produce high-quality DO wines.

Beer is popular, with San Miguel, Mahou and Cruzcampo among the most popular brands. That said, more and more small, independent breweries are popping up along the coast, and *cervezas artesanales* (craft beers) are booming. Try La Socarrada beer from Xátiva (lasocarrada.com), with its notes of

INSIDER TIP
Delicious honey beer

honey and rosemary for a sweet aftertaste. The brewers of Cerveza Gènesis *(cervezagenesis.com)* in Favara near València add orange juice to their beer, and the pioneering DeBassus pub brewery *(cervezadebassus.com)* in Orihuela Costa produces beer with hops and malt straight from Bavaria.

After a meal, reach for a glass of the grape must liqueur *(mistela)* as a digestif or the extremely sweet herbal liqueur *43* from Cartagena.

TODAY'S SPECIALS

Snacks

BOCADILLOS
Sandwiches on white bread, filled with ham, cheese or tortilla

BOQUERONES EN VINAGRE
Anchovies marinated in vinegar and a dash of olive oil

GAMBAS AL AJILLO
Prawns fried in garlic, olive oil and a little chilli, served in a ceramic bowl

Starters

PAN I AIOLI
White bread served with olive oil, garlic, salt and lemon

GAZPACHO
Cold soup made of uncooked tomatoes, served with chopped onions, cucumber, peppers and croutons

Main courses

PAELLA VALENCIANA
Rice dish with chicken, rabbit, peppers, tomato, garlic, a hint of saffron and paprika

ARROZ NEGRO
Rice dish with onions, peppers, calamari and prawns, cooked in squid ink

LENGUADO
Fried sole served with potatoes and green veg

ATÚN EN ESCABECHE
Tuna marinated in vinegar

CHULETAS DE CORDERO
Lamb chops with garlic and rosemary

Desserts

FLAN
Pudding made from egg, milk and caramelised sugar and cooked in a water bath

TURRÓN
Spanish nougat made from almonds, honey, sugar and egg whites

Digestifs

CARAJILLO
Espresso with brandy

MISTELA
Sweet liqueur made from grape must

SHOPPING

Hoping to take home a taste of Spain? No problem! Whether you prefer liqueurs and sweet wines from Benicàssim or Xaló, nougat *(turrón)* from Xixona or capers *(alcaparras)* from Águilas, Spain's southeast coast is famed far and wide for its delicacies. Or there are ceramics and clothes for a more permanent souvenir.

FOR THE FOODIES

Cold-pressed olive oil *(aceite de oliva virgen extra)* can be bought almost everywhere, including at roadside stands. An easy-to-transport option is 🚩 *chorizo*, a hearty, and importantly dried, sausage flavoured with paprika and garlic – or you could opt for a good cheese like the famous hard cheese from the region of La Mancha *(queso manchego)*. You should also take the opportunity to buy air-dried Serrano ham – it is two to three times less expensive than at home. Quick tip: choose to have hams, sausages and cheeses sealed in plastic *(envasar al vacío)* so they keep better!

ISLAND CERAMICS

Ceramics have always been a popular souvenir and were originally brought to the Levant coast by the Moors. Pottery shops in Peñíscola, around Calp and in Guadalest on the Costa Blanca sell handmade jugs and vases with unique designs; you will also find what you are looking for near Alicante and Agost. The cork and metal flasks made in the area around Sagunt make decorative souvenirs. The upright version is known as a *colcho* (masculine), while the horizontal version is known as a *colcha* (feminine), suggesting some questionable gender stereotypes.

From food to fashion, València is a shopper's paradise

FASHION & ACCESSORIES

Does the name Amancio Ortega mean anything to you? Probably not – although our guess is you probably know his shops. After all, he's the founder of a fashion empire that includes the chains Zara, Pull & Bear, Bershka and Massimo Dutti, among others. Ortega features on Forbes' top ten list of the richest individuals in the world, and he tops the rich list in Spain. No wonder, since his fashion shops dominate the streets of even the smallest towns in Spain. That said, there are plenty of alternatives: Desigual or Custo for the trend-conscious with a larger budget, or Mango or Springfield for those with a little less cash at hand. In the old town of Altea, small designers sell more individual fashion and accessories, both in their stores and at summer street markets. Meanwhile, the hinterland of the Costa Blanca is well known for its shoe factories.

INSIDER TIP
Not off the peg

Pottery from València

SPORT & ACTIVITIES

The Spanish Mediterranean coast offers something for every sports enthusiast, whether that's hiking, cycling, golfing, windsurfing, kite-surfing or something else entirely. Potentially even better are the unique sports that are only available here, like diving down to the shipwrecks at Cabo de Palos, kayaking across the Mar Menor or ballooning over the lunar landscape near Elche.

BALLOONING

Aeroglobo (tel. 9 66 63 74 01 | aero globo.com) lies south of Elche; the balloon flights start at 8am at weekends, ascending to a maximum altitude of 1000m. Prices (approx. 150 euros/pers.) include picnic and diploma. Further inland, Bocairent, north-west of Alcoi, is the home base of *Tot Globo (Els Clots | tel. 6 29 61 18 89 | totglobo.com)*. Take an hour to let the wind carry you over the mountains and plains below, the Mediterranean never far from view on the horizon.

CYCLING

Spain might be a nation of cyclists, but cycling cannot be recommended everywhere in Spain: the cycle paths are often either in poor condition or do not exist at all; this, together with the partly heavy traffic and often inconsiderate drivers tend to reduce the pleasure of cycling in town. That said, more and more bike paths are cropping up in towns along the coast, especially in the tourist strongholds of Benidorm and La Manga. What can also be recommended are the *Vías Verdes (via-verdes.com)*, "Green Routes", which run on the former tracks of narrow-gauge railway lines or along planned train routes, such as the *Vía*

INSIDER TIP
A two-wheel dream

Strange encounters take place underwater

Verde de Ojos Negros, which runs for 68km between Barracas (province of Castellón) and Algimia de Alfara (province of València). Shorter stretches can be found in Alicante Province, such as the *Vía Verde de Maigmó* between Agost and the 660-m-high Puerto del Maigmó (22 km), as well as the *Vía Verde del Xixarra 2* between the Santuario de las Virtudes and Biar (15km). Mountain bikers will like the route near the coast through the Serra d'Irta Nature Reserve from Peñíscola to Alcossebre/Alcocebre. Spanish law requires cyclists to wear a helmet.

DIVING

There are many diving schools on the Costa Blanca. These include *Revolution Dive (Edificio Comodoro | Local 61 | Puerto Deportivo Luis Campomanes | tel. 9 65 85 29 74 | revolutiondive. com)* near Altea and the *Centro de Buceo Dive & Dive (Club Naútico |* *Av. del Puerto | tel. 9 65 83 92 70 | divedivecompany.com)* in Calp. In Mar Menor, there are several diving centres, including the *Club de Buceo Islas Hormigas (Paseo de la Barra s/n | Cabo de Palos | tel. 6 20 55 79 40 | islas hormigas.com)* which is open all year round. In one of their most exciting tours, divers can go down to **INSIDER TIP** **Diving thrills** see the wrecks around the Islas Hormigas, where various ships have met their watery fate.

GOLF

There are several 18-hole, par 72 courses near Alicante, including the *Club de Golf Alenda (Av. del Mediterráneo 52 | Monforte del Cid | tel. 965620521 | alendagolf.com)*, the *Club de Golf Alicante (Av. Locutor Vicente Hipólito 37 | Playa de San Juan | tel. 9 65 15 37 94 | alicantegolf.com)* and *Romero Golf* near Pilar de la

Horadada *(Ctra. Orihuela, km 29, CV 925 | Pilar de la Horadada | tel. 9 66 76 68 87 | loromerogolf.com)*. Green fees can be booked online for various clubs at the informative *golfcostablanca.org*.

INSIDER TIP
Golfing in style

One of the most beautiful courses in Spain – a world of its own with beautiful greens under palm trees and a treasure trove of small lakes – is located to the south of the Mar Menor: the *La Manga Club (Ctra. Atamaria Cartgena | tel. 9 68 33 12 34 | lamangaclub.es)*. The vast complex is complete with five-star hotel, four-star apartments, three world-famous golf courses, a 28-court tennis centre, eight football pitches, a cricket ground and a 2,000-m² wellness centre. Plus, there are more than a dozen restaurants offering almost any cuisine you could dream of.

HIKING

The Costa del Azahar, Costa Blanca and Costa Cálida are a hiker's paradise. The most popular hiking areas are the nature reserves such as the Serra d'Irta near Peñíscola, El Montgó near Dénia, the Penyal d'Ifac near Calp, the Sierra Helada near Benidorm and the Parque Regional de Calblanque near Cartagena. Beautiful and well-marked hiking trails are also an option inland, such as the Sierra Helada and the Sierra de Bérnia near Callosa d'en Sarrià. For a truly stunning hike, circumnavigate the Sierra de Bérnia (3½ hrs). Start the tour at the Casas de Bérnia on the northern side. From there, the trail leads up into the Forat de Bérnia, a 50-m-long rock tunnel, including a 10-m passage that can only be done on hands and knees. The sunny southwestern slope reveals fabulous views of Altea Bay before you pass the ruins of the Fort de Bérnia to return to the starting point.

KAYAKING

The Mar Menor is simply *the* place to go for kayakers. The *Escuela de Vela Sandrina (Gran Vía, km 6 | Edificio Orfeo | La Manga del Mar Menor | tel. 9 68 14 13 27 | Facebook: escuela sandrina)* has its headquarters right on the shores of the Mar Menor. The school does not limit itself to sailing; it also rents out kayaks to people who want to explore a section of the inland sea on their own. Another recommended address is the *La Bocana (Paseo Libertat s/n | tel. 6 56 90 19 78 | labocana.es)* sports centre in the Marina Salinas port of Torrevieja. The *Centro de Deportes Náuticos Las Antípodas (Ctra. Calp–Moraira, km 2 | tel. 6 65 85 32 00 | lasantipodas.com)* near Calp also rents kayaks and organises excursions.

SAILING

The sailing and boat clubs *(clubs náuticos)* sometimes organise sailing courses for beginners and advanced sailors alike – also for children from the age of 7. *Real Club Náutico de Calp (Av. Puerto Pesquero s/n | Calp | tel. 9 65 83 18 09 | rcnc.es)*, the *Club Náutico de Santa Pola (Muelle Poniente | Santa Pola | tel. 9 65 41 24 03 | cnauticosantapola.com)* and the *Real Club Náutico de Torrevieja (Paseo Vistalegre | Torrevieja | tel. 9 65 71 01 12 | rcnt. com)*.

WINDSURFING & SUP

Windsurfers will find excellent spots on the Costa Blanca northwest of Dénia. The area *La Chimenea-Les Deveses* is well-known for its reliable strong winds (speeds 3.5–7). This is the location of centres such as the *Windcenter Dénia (Camí del Bassot | Playa Les Deveses | tel. 9 65 75 53 07 | windcenter denia.com)*. In El Campello northeast of Alicante, you will find the *Campello Surf Club (campellosurfclub. com)* which also offers beginner courses in the summer. Stand-up paddleboarding is also on offer. Kitesurfers can book courses via the *Escola Valenciana Kitesurf (Playa del Brosquil | Cullera | tel. 6 44 21 53 41 | evk-escolavalencianakitesurf.blogspot.com); the Radical Surf School (Calle Madrid 2 | Cullera | tel. 6 07 30 66 61 | radical windsurf.com)*, specialised in wind- and kitesurfing is based in Cullera. SUP fans, meanwhile, will fall in love with the inland sea of Mar Menor.

YOGA

Relax, detox and enjoy: yoga is growing in popularity far beyond Ibiza, *the* destination for yoga, and has long since made it to the southeast coast of Spain. *La Crisalida Retreat (Av. de Sant Marc 9 | tel. 9 66 86 52 42 | lacrisalida retreats.com)* near Albir on the Costa Blanca is a beautiful retreat whether you just need a break from the daily grind, are hoping to detox your body or just want to spend a few days at peace. This retreat does it all. They also offer a whole range of courses and workshops – everything from yoga to detox and weight loss.

There are spectacular hiking routes through the Sierra Helada

REGIONAL OVERVIEW

Embalse de Buendia

Rio Tajo

Rio Guadiana

Rio Guadalquivir

Crystal-clear water, plenty of sun and the holiday factory of La Manga

50 km
31.07 mi

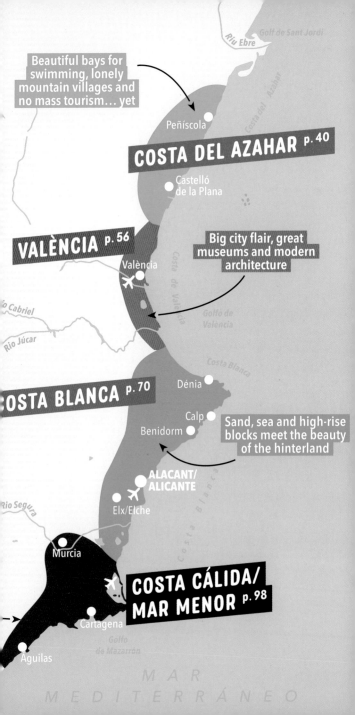

Beautiful bays for swimming, lonely mountain villages and no mass tourism… yet

Peñíscola

COSTA DEL AZAHAR p. 40

Castelló de la Plana

VALÈNCIA p. 56

Big city flair, great museums and modern architecture

València

Golfo de Valencia

COSTA BLANCA p. 70

Dénia

Calp

Benidorm

Sand, sea and high-rise blocks meet the beauty of the hinterland

ALACANT/ ALICANTE

Elx/Elche

Murcia

COSTA CÁLIDA/ MAR MENOR p. 98

Cartagena

Aguilas

Golfo de Mazarrón

MAR MEDITERRÁNEO

Riu Ebre

Golf de Sant Jordi

Costa del Azahar

Costa de Valencia

Costa Blanca

Costa Blanca

Río Cabriel

Río Júcar

Río Segura

COSTA DEL AZAHAR

QUIET TOWNS, FANTASTIC BEACHES

The most beautiful time to visit is in April and May, when the Costa del Azahar, "Orange Blossom Coast", lives up to its name, and the flowering trees (*azahar* in Spanish) exude a bewitching perfume. But there's also plenty to see and enjoy on this stretch of coastline during the other ten months of the year.

After all, unlike other parts of the Spanish coast, the Costa del Azahar is hardly known abroad, meaning mass tourism hasn't completely taken over here. This stretch of the coast has all the

The old town of Peñíscola enjoys a prime position on the coast

ingredients for a perfect holiday: the secluded beach at Torre la Sal is the ideal counterpoint to the lively beach promenade of Benicàssim. The enchanting old town of Peñíscola towers high above the Mediterranean while the unspoiled mountain village of Vilafamés is an attractive alternative in the hinterland. But the biggest contrast is the difference between the touristy town of Marina d'Or, pumping out hotels and guests, and the pure beauty of nature reserves like the Serra d'Irta. You will be amazed!

COSTA DEL AZAHAR

Vallibona

N232

Xe

226

La Iglesuela del Cid

Castellfort

Catí

Sant Mateu

16

Ares del Maestrat

Tírig

Vilafranca / Villafranca del Cid

COMUNITAT VALENCIANA

ARAGÓN

Benassal

Albocàsser

10

les Coves de Vinromà

Vistabella del Maestrat

la Torre d'en Besora

Benafigós

15

la Torre d'en Domènec

58km, 40 mins

Xodos / Chodos

Atzeneta del Maestrat

Vall d'Alba

N340

les Useres / Useras

Cabanes

Torre la Sal 5

Llucena / Lucena del Cid

Vilafamés ★ 9

Orpesa 6 **Platja
la Conc**

Ludiente

Desert de les Palmes ★ 7

Platja Almadrava

l'Alcora

Benicàssim(Benicasim)
p.49

Platja Torre Sant Vicen

Ribesalbes

16

Beaches at Benicà

Ayódar

20

Río Millars

37km, 35 mins

8 **Castelló de la Plana**

21

Onda

Vila-real

Betxí

A7

Alcúdia de Veo

Borriana

55km, 2¾ hrs

Artana

Chóvar

Nules

GOLF DE

Coves de Sant Josep 10

La Vall d'Uixó

VALENCIA

Algar de Palancia

N225

Moncofa

N340

la Llosa

Sant Rafel del Riu
Ulldecona
Sant Carles de la Ràpita
N340
Alcanar
Costa de Fora
Traiguera
N232
N238
ervera del Maestre
Vinaròs 2
1 Benicarló
Old town ★
Playa Norte
N340
Peñíscola
p. 44
3 Serra d'Irta Nature Reserve ★

4 Alcossebre

MARCO POLO HIGHLIGHTS

★ PEÑÍSCOLA OLD TOWN
The walled district on the way up
towards the castle still exudes a village
atmosphere ➤ p. 44

★ SERRA D'IRTA NATURE RESERVE
Cliffs, beaches, hiking paths and
marvellous views south of Peñíscola
➤ p. 48

★ BEACHES AT BENICÀSSIM
Sandy capital with bonus promenades –
the most beautiful beaches are Voramar,
Almadrava and Torre Sant Vicent ➤ p. 51

★ DESERT DE LES PALMES /
DESIERTO DE LAS PALMAS
The rugged mountain world behind
Benicàssim ➤ p. 52

★ VILAFAMÉS
Unspoilt village in the hinterland with
castle ruins and rural accommodation
➤ p. 54

11 Illes Columbretes

10 km
6.21 mi

PENÍSCOLA

(□□ G3) **Seen** *Pirates of the Caribbean* **recently? Affording a unique view of the entire coast of the Mediterranean, the fortified old-town promontory of Peñíscola (pop. 7,600) juts out into the sea high above the harbour and beaches, making it the perfect backdrop for some pirate-inspired adventures.**

Square, whitewashed houses are staggered up to the highest plateau of the rocky hillock, which is dominated by a mediaeval fortress. The newly constructed areas of the city spread out away from the historical heart of Peñíscola. Sand filling made it possible to extend the North Beach as far as the neighbouring village of Benicarló; palm-lined promenades invite visitors to take strolls in their shade.

SIGHTSEEING

OLD TOWN ★ ⚑

Peñíscola claims to have the most beautiful Old Town on the entire Costa del Azahar: the 16th-century walls surround a mountain spur. You'd better be in good shape to conquer the old town and the castle, but it's worth the effort: stone-paved streets, small shops and boutiques, cosy tapas bars and fish restaurants and, yes, the castle complete with breath-taking view over the turquoise Mediterranean Sea at the end all help make Peñíscola one of the most picturesque places on the entire coast. From the port, visitors

are swallowed up by the *Portal de Sant Pere*, a city gate with the C/ Atarazanas rising up behind it. This is where you will find the blow-hole that fizzes and hisses and sprays when there are high waves and rough seas. You make your way upwards over warped paving through a complex system of narrow lanes. The C/ Nou will overwhelm you with its lush floral glory; in the distance, you will catch a glimpse of the sea; small bars and restaurants line the way. The castle and small lighthouse occupy the highest point at around 65m above sea level. One leaves or enters the Old Town from the North Beach side through the steep *Subida Portal Fosc*.

CASTLE

This fortress with its battlements was erected by the Knights Templar between 1294 and 1307 on the site of a former Moorish complex. At the time of the so-called "Western Schism", the splitting of the church that lasted from 1378 to 1417, antipope Benedict XIII sought refuge in the castle at Peñíscola. His real name was Pedro de Luna; he came from Aragon and was ultimately unsuccessful in his attempt to take over control of the Catholic Church. He managed to survive many attempts made to poison him before dying at (an estimated) 80 years of age in 1423. His body was temporarily entombed in the castle church and the bare room he died in can be visited today. The castle is also known as "Papa Luna" in honour of its most famous former resident; the labyrinthine complex, which even includes a dungeon, has

Antipope Benedict XIII took shelter in Peñíscola's castle at the turn of the 15th century

been painstakingly restored. There are magnificent views over the beaches and mountains from the esplanade and lookout platforms. *Daily 10.30am–5.30pm, in summer, daily 9.30am–9.30pm | Plaza de Armas | castillode peniscola.dipcas.es |* ⏱ *2 hrs.*

CASA DE LAS CONCHAS

At some point in our lives, we've all picked up a shell or two from the beach to take home as a prized souvenir. But how many trips must Tomiteo and Justa have made to collect enough shells to adorn the front of their house from top to bottom in nature's decorations? The couple are said to have lived in the Old Town of Peñíscola in the 1950s, and to earn some money, they started guiding travellers around their home town. They are the "Adam and Eve" of city guides, so to speak, and the façade of their house in Calle Faraones 11 could even be seen as an early tourist promotion campaigns.

FISHING PORT

The fishing port *(puerto pesquero)* is an inviting place to take a stroll, with splendid views of the walled castle in the Old Town and the hills behind. In addition, an exceedingly busy fishing fleet has its home here. Depending on the season, weather and success of the catch, the fishermen come back to port between 4pm and 5pm from Monday to Friday and that is when the fish auction begins. Visitors can watch them unloading their boats and the auctions, which are not open to the general public, are held at the long *Llotja de peix* building. The *Bar Puerto Mar (Facebook: restaurantpuertomar)* is a good place to relax and enjoy fish straight from the sea.

JARDÍN DEL PAPAGAYO

Follow the wild screeching to the "Parrot Garden" – home to some 500 colourful birds. The overgrown, park-like area contains many aviaries, which you can enter – but beware of "dive bombers". What is more, there are flight shows *(exhibiciones)* of parrots, a butterfly house *(Butterfly Fort)*, the kangaroo zone and the "adventure" area *(Aventura)* for all those who would like to practise balancing acts. *From 11am with various closing times according to the season: 3pm in winter and 8pm in summer | admission 16 euros, children (3–12 years) 12 euros | Camino del Término Peñíscola–Benicarló (signposted from Peñíscola) | jardindelpapagayo.com | ⏱ 1½ hrs.*

EATING & DRINKING

CASA DOROTEA

This restaurant is the place to go in the Old Town for a good meal in an informal setting: the speciality of the house is the excellent homemade paella. There are also a few tables and chairs outside on the pavement. Simple but authentic. *Closed Tue | Oct-March only open for lunch on Sat/Sun | C/ San Vicente 12 | tel. 9 64 48 08 63 | €*

INSIDER TIP
Poetry in a pan!

TIO PEPE

On the busiest street in the centre of town; a good selection ranging from black rice to a fish platter. Popular with the locals. If it is too full for you, there

Unloading the day's catch in Peñíscola's harbour

are plenty of alternatives nearby. *Daily, closed on Sun evenings in winter | Av. España 32 | tel. 9 64 48 06 40 | €€*

SHOPPING

FRUTAS PIÑANA

A gigantic shop with freshly harvested fruit and vegetables and the best prices far and wide. Ideal for those who are catering for themselves or have driven here and want to take a crate of juicy oranges back home with them. *Av. Papa Luna 146 | the car park can only be reached from the rear | frutaspiñana.com*

BEACHES

The small town boasts fine, sandy beaches that live up to the hype. The main area is the 🏖 *Playa Norte* (North Beach); it stretches for miles and is well provided with showers, children's playground equipment and beach-volleyball nets. The small *Playa Sur* (South Beach) near the fishing port is actually rather attractive but cannot be recommended for swimming.

SPORT & ACTIVITIES

The beach promenade towards Benicarló is popular with joggers. There is also a lane for cyclists; bikes can be hired from *Bicicletas Freddy (Av. Papa Luna 79 | Edificio Marina | tel. 6 37 28 50 50), Diver-Sport (Av. Estación 7 | tel. 6 33 97 97 42 | diversport.net)* and elsewhere. In the high season,

excursion boats or *golodrinas* set sail from the fishing harbour for half-hour trips around the promontory with its historic Old Town.

NIGHTLIFE

Things can become rather lively on the promenade near the North Beach and in the area around the main street, Av. España. However, Peñíscola is more of a destination for families so it does not have a great choice of nightlife. One exception is the *Ebano (discoteca ebano.com)* nightclub near the sea front.

AROUND PEÑÍSCOLA

1 BENICARLÓ
8km / 13 mins by car via the CV-140
This small, neighbouring town (pop. 27,000) to the north has a busy port and is mainly attractive as an alternative to spending your holiday in Peñíscola. Of interest in March is *Las Fallas* with its gigantic constructions, which can be seen all around the town. Try the *Hogar del Pescador (Av. Marquès de Benicarló 29, on the corner of C/Cristo del Mar | tel. 9 64 96 58 05 | hogardelpescador benicarlo.es | €–€€)* for an excellent fish meal. ▥ *G3*

2 VINARÒS (VINAROZ)
21km / 20 mins by car via the N-340
It is worth visiting this small town on

There are far-reaching views of the Serra d'Irta from Castillo de Xivert

the coast (pop. 29,000) to the north to see the bustling fishing port and the market near the promenade *(mercadillo seminal)* where all kinds of things are sold on Thursday morning. The most attractive beach is named *Fortí*. The centrally located *Los Arcos Restaurant (closed Wed | Paseo Colón 9 | tel. 9 64 45 56 72 | €–€€)* serves good tapas, rice and fish dishes, and a reasonably priced (slightly more expensive on weekends) daily set menu. *G2–3*

🔳 SERRA D'IRTA NATURE RESERVE ★

11km / 30 mins by car via Vía Polígono 8
South of Peñíscola, running parallel to the coast, the hills of the Serra d'Irta (also Sierra de Hirta) rise up to a height of 573m. Cliffs, pine trees and brush-covered slopes alternate with

secluded beaches. The small *Playa el Russo* and *Playa el Pebret* beaches can only be reached from Peñíscola via a wide bumpy road – with the exception of one small surfaced section – so can only be recommended for sturdy vehicles. The alternative is a lengthy hike. You will pass the *Torre Abadum*, a mediaeval Moorish fortified tower. It is no longer permitted to climb up the tower but you will be able to admire the marvellous views of the Mediterranean from all around its base. If you think your car is up to it, you can take the bumpy coastal road from Russo or Pebret to Alcossebre (deep ruts, dust and gravel!). There are also some castle ruins and the former *Sant Antoni* hermitage high up in the mountains.

Many hiking paths traverse the nature reserve (see Discovery Tour 3 p. 118), and the tourist information office can provide you with a general map; alternatively, you can visit the homepage of the community *(penis-cola.es)* to download maps under the heading "Nature".

Speaking of hiking, ever had a castle to yourself for a mid-hike break? Why not try out the castle lifestyle for yourself in the Sierra d'Irta near Alcalà de Xivert where the Castillo de Xivert rises defiantly above the Sierra d'Irta. The journey takes 20 minutes by car over a mixed surfaced/dirt bumpy road (7km) or two hours hiking from Alcalà de Xivert (4km,

ER TIP
Your very own castle

sharp ascents in places), and during the week you'll almost always have the place

to yourself. Plus, the view over the Serra d'Irta and the village of Alcalà de Xivert is just stunning: note the 68-m-high bell tower on the church of Sant Joan Baptista. *G3*

4 ALCOSSEBRE (ALCOCÉBER)
32km / 30 mins by car via the N-340
Unpretentious, quiet and relaxing. Alcossebre is an extended coastal community (pop. 7,000) on the southwestern flank of the Serra d'Irta. It might not be a gem in terms of urban planning, but it's a favourite with tourists who love to holiday in the town's small hotels and villas – not least because it's largely been spared the raging stampedes of tourists that plague other beaches further south on the coast. The most attractive beaches – Romana, Cargador and Las Fuentes – are situated close to the centre. *G3*

5 TORRE LA SAL
44km / 40 mins by car via the N-340
At just 250m long, this sleepy town probably has the shortest beach promenade on the whole Orange Blossom Coast. Made up of just four streets, it's so small that it can be tricky to pinpoint on a map, and despite having the tourist hotspot Marina d'Or just next door, you end up feeling like you're miles away from civilization. Thankfully there's also a simple bar *(Dolce Vita | €)* and even a restaurant: the *Casa Artemio (€–€€)*. An added bonus is the charming and mostly deserted *Parc Natural Prat de Cabanes-Torreblanca*, whose marshes stretch alongside the coast. *G*

BENICÀSSIM

(F4) **The intriguing name of the small town of Benicàssim (pop. 18,000), which covers a wide area approx. 80km north of València, is of Arabic origin; the Moors and Christians waged many violent battles in this area between the 11th and 13th centuries.**

In later centuries, the coast was subject to attack by pirates; the watchtower from the 16th century behind the Platja Torre Sant Vicent was once part of an extensive defence system with almost 20 similar towers. Starting at the end of the 19th century, well-off Valencians became the next to lay siege to Benicàssim – they were the forerunners of modern-day tourists and had magnificent villas built

Arenal Sound in Burriana

behind the beaches where they idled away their long summers. This developed into the "Valencian Biarritz". The wide sandy beaches and pleasant climate are still the main assets of Benicàssim, and the historical villas are now listed as protected buildings.

SIGHTSEEING

BODEGAS CARMELITANO

The production of these tasty tipples including the famous *licor carmelitano* can be traced back to the Carmelite monks who established the monastery in Benicàssim at the beginning of the 18th century. It is made of a carefully guarded "miracle recipe" consisting of around 40 different herbs. Visitors taking part in the tours of the time-honoured cellars, distillery

and bottling plant will be almost overpowered by the sweetish aroma. Nowadays, the operation is no longer run by the monks but by normal workers. Some of the massive oak barrels can contain 4000 litres (880 gallons). The current entrance fee of 3.60 euros includes a sample at the end of the tour. You will be able to try the sweet "communion wine", muscatel, and apple, hazelnut and Carmelite liqueurs. The shop sells the entire range of products at reasonable prices. *Daily 9am–1.30pm and 3.30–7pm | C. Bodolz 12 | carmelitano.com | ⏱ 1 hr*

EATING & DRINKING

CASA VICENTE

This family-run restaurant is very popular with the locals, especially for its exceptional paella! It's also a good spot for breakfast but there's no dinner service. *Daily 9am–3pm | Plaça La Estación 8 | tel. 9 64 30 12 49 | €*

MESÓN LA ESTAFETA

Elegant ambience with a rustic interior decorated with a lot of wood; near the centre. The house specialises in typical Mediterranean cuisine with the main focus on rice dishes. *Closed Mon | Paseo Pérez Bayer 35 | tel. 9 64 30 21 81 | mesonestafeta.com | Moderate| €€*

BEACHES

The most beautiful beaches in Benicàssim start at Avenida Barcelona and on the coastal road respectively and are separated from each other by breakwaters: ★ ⚑ *Platja Voramar, Platja Almadrava* and *Platja Torre San Vicent*. The beaches are wide and covered with fine sand, with magnificent promenades running parallel to them. The smaller *Platja Els Terrers* and the long *Platja Heliópolis* continue farther to the south, but here the view is impaired by the ugly skyline of the commercial port of Castelló de la Plana.

SPORT & ACTIVITIES

In summer, water-lovers are drawn to the large pool landscapes of the *Aquarama (mid-June–beginning of Sept daily 10am–7pm | Ctra. N-340, km 987 | aquarama.net)* aquatic park with its slides and other attractions.

The municipal *indoor swimming pool* can be found in the C/ Torre Sant Vicent 41. The long seafront promenade means that Benicàssim is wonderful for cycling.

INSIDER TIP
Two-wheeled tour

The short ride (5.5km) along the "Green Route" (*Vía Verde*) to Oropesa del Mar is very beautiful. What might be expensive elsewhere is free in Benicassìm, where there is ⚑ free bike rental. Well, on the condition you are at least 18 years old, have an ID with you and are prepared to leave a 50 euro deposit. Pick up bikes from the *Pabellón de Deportes (Mon–Sat 9am–2pm and 4–9pm, Sun 9am–2pm | C/ Torre de Sant Vicent s/n | tel. 9 64 30 26 62).*

HIP FESTIVALS

Every year in July, 40,000 visitors make the pilgrimage to the FIB. The *Festival Internacional de Benicàssim (fiberfib.com)* hosts four days of independent rock and pop concerts across multiple stages. Benicàssim is also home to one of Europe's biggest reggae festivals, *Rototom Sunsplash (Facebook: rototom sunsplashofficial)*. For a week in August reggae fans won't get a moment's rest! As if that weren't enough, it's not just bands but world-famous DJs who take to the stage at *Arenal Sound (arenal sound.com)* in Burriana, south of Castelló. This festival also runs over several days (July/Aug) and draws tens of thousands of music lovers.

NIGHTLIFE

The most popular pubs where people meet to spend the evening hours are along the central streets – Avenida da Castelló and Avenida Santo Tomás – as well as behind the Platja Sant Vicent and around the Plaça dels Dolors.

AROUND BENICÀSSIM

🔟 ORPESA (OROPESA DEL MAR)
10km / 12 mins by car via the N-340
The small village (pop. 9,000) is divided into three sections: the Old Town, the coastal village and the Marina d'Or holiday village. The remains of the castle in the Old Town can be visited, free of charge, during the day. Its origins can be traced back to Muslim rule and it was also in the hands of the Knights Hospitaller in the Middle Ages. The Chapel of Mary *Virgen de la Paciencia* (18th century), the *Museo del Naipe (open daily, 10.30am to 1.30pm, otherwise only with prior reservation | tel. 6 26 56 47 49 | C/ Hospital 1 | museo delnaipe.com)* with a collection of playing cards and the *Museo del Hierro (July/Aug, Tues–Sun 10am–2pm | C/ Ramón y Cajal)* which is only open in the summer offering an exhibition of wrought iron artistic objects and two historical defence towers: the *Torre del Rey* and the *Torre de Corda*.

The most beautiful beach is the sweeping, shell-shaped *✦ Platja de la Concha*. This is also where you can find the *Hotel Marina (17 rooms | Paseo Marítimo La Concha | tel. 9 64 31 00 99 | hotel marina.com.es | €)*; the restaurant is also popular with people not staying at the hotel. The marina is at the southern end of Platja de la Concha while a path in the opposite direction leads past the lighthouse promontory to the *Morro de Gos* and *Les Amplàries* beaches as well as the coastal monster *Marina d'Or* with all of its architectural eyesores. *Marina d'Or (marinador.com)* even boasts that it is the 'largest leisure and holiday city in Europe'. This might be an exaggeration but there are certainly more than enough sparkling lights, kitsch and hullabaloo. This is where you can find hotels and health complexes, holiday flats, a park for children, restaurants, bars and discos. Gardens are laid out in neo-modernist style and footbridges lead down to the beach. Of course, there are also all kinds of events. ◫ *F–G4*

🔟 DESERT DE LES PALMES (DESIERTO DE LAS PALMAS) ★
9km / 20 mins by car via the CV-147
A nature reserve for even the most outdoor averse whose name means "palm desert". Even if the name "desert", which symbolises the solitude of the place, is misleading, the nature reserve in the hinterland of the Benicàssim is a sure-fire hit. The mountains here rise to an altitude of 729m and were where Carmelite monks withdrew centuries ago. The monastery we see today dates from the 18th century and is located on a

A hand-decorated façade in Castelló de la Plana

lovely mountain road; signposted from Benicàssim. After you leave the motorway behind you, you drive up the curving CV-147 country road into the mountains; this route is also very popular with cyclists. Contrary to the name, common plants in the area are pines, arbutus and various hardy herbs. Along the way, there are several places where you can park your car and admire the splendid panoramic views of the Mediterranean and to Benicàssim. The monastery itself is less attractive and it is the landscape which takes centre stage. A hike to the castle on a rock, *Castillo de Montornés* (starting point on the road), is another interesting activity in the mountains. *F–G4*

⑧ CASTELLÓ DE LA PLANA (CASTELLÓN DE LA PLANA)

15km / 19 mins by car on the CV-149
Let's be honest, there are not many buildings of historical interest in this provincial capital (pop. 170,000) south of Benicàssim. Beyond the 17th-century bell tower of the *Concatredral de Santa María* and the *Basílica de Santa María del Lledo* just outside the city centre, the city has little else to offer. On the other hand, the *market halls* not far away, with their fish, sausage and cheese selections are actually much more interesting.

In the middle of the 13th century, it was decided to move the city from the nearby mountain slopes down to the coastal plain La Plana. The colourful annual festival *Festes de la Magdalena* commemorates this event in March (occasionally continuing into April) with processions, fireworks, folklore and an accompanying culinary programme.

Local cultural centres include the theatre and the modern Espai d'Art Contemporani (eacc. es); here you get the chance to meet dedicated young artists, musicians and filmmakers as well as attend free workshops. If you're on a budget, head to the free 🐦 *Museu Belles Arts (Tue–Sat 10am–2pm, 4–8pm, Sun 10am–2pm | Av. Hermanos Bou 28 | ⏱ 1 hr)*, the museum of fine arts, where the walls are adorned with works by Francisco de Osona, Juan de Juanes, Juan Ribalta and Francisco de Zurbarán, among others. Similarly, painters like Gabriel Puig Roda, Vicent Castell Domènech and Joan Baptista Torcar have captured popular scenes, while additional rooms feature sculptures and Valencian ceramics as well as interesting archaeological and folklore exhibits.

The port of *El Grao*, a few miles to the east of the city centre, is also part of Castelló de la Plana. The *Planetarium (Passeig Marítim 1 | Grao de Castelló | tel. 9 64 2 82 96)* looms up out of the not exactly edifying panorama. ⌕ *F4*

🟨 VILAFAMÉS ★
37km / 35 mins by car via the N-340 and CV-10
This hamlet (pop. 1,900) northwest of Benicàssim is one of the most

beautiful places in the hinterland of the Costa del Azahar. Vilafamés is built across several ledges on the slopes and there is a spectacular panoramic view from the highest point by the castle ruins. You should park your car in the lower section of the village or at the open car park in front of the Assumpció Renaissance church and then walk. Narrow streets with quarry stone buildings and hanging plants are set off against the whitewashed facades of the houses in the village. The *Hotel El Rullo (C/ La Fuente 2 | tel. 9 64 32 93 84 | elrullo.es | €)* is a centrally located place to stay, complete with a rustic restaurant serving an appealing menu. This small community is full of surprises, however: Vilafamés may have fewer than 2,000 residents and yet it boasts a wonderful little art museum, the Museu d'Art Contemporani, named

for its founder Vicente Aguilar Cerni *(Tue–Sun 10am–2pm and 4–6.30pm | C/ Diputació 20 | macvac.es).* ▢ F4

🔟 COVES DE SANT JOSEP (GRUTAS DE SAN JOSÉ) 🏊

49km / 40 mins by car via the AP-7
Jump into the boat, keep your head down and then marvel at the bizarre stalactites and stalagmites as you glide along a subterranean river. Boatsmen punt you along passages and into cave chambers such as the "Cathedral" and "Bat Hall". The most important nooks and crannies are illuminated, and part of the tour is on foot. *Tour ⏱ 40–45 minutes | daily 10am–3pm, June–Sept to 6.30pm | admission 10 euros, children (up to 1.01 m and max 13 years) 5 euros | on the outskirts of La Vall d'Uixó, signposted access, large car park | riosubterraneo.com |* ▢ E–F5

11 ILLES COLUMBRETES (ISLAS COLUMBRETES)

46km / 2 hrs by boat from Benicassìm
Once again, Captain Sparrow sends his greetings! This archipelago around 30 sea miles off the coast was once known only to pirates, smugglers and fishermen. The rugged island world is protected by law and there are strict rules in place for the few visitors allowed to visit the main island every day. The Columbretes are a popular destination for diving excursions or boating – if you like boating and are in the mood for a deserted island, why not let yourself drift! Day trips are offered from starting points including Castelló, Benicàssim, Orpesa and Peñíscola: *visitaislascolumbretes.com |* ▢ H4–5

INSIDER TIP
Island isolation

Lighthouse on Illes Grossa, the largest of the Islas Columbretes

VALÈNCIA

URBAN FLAIR & MODERN ARCHITECTURE

València – it even sounds beautiful! There is a special music to the name. The Romans and Moors felt magnetically drawn to the city and left their mark on this Mediterranean metropolis.

In 1094, the Spanish national hero El Cid advanced on the city and wrested it from the Muslims for the first time. However, it was not until 1238 that King Jaume I completed the Christian reconquest Since then, agriculture and trade have helped the city to gain pros perity; today it is tourism that keeps the cash registers ringing.

Ciutat de les Arts i les Ciències in València

The catastrophic flooding of the Turia river in 1957 led to the "Plan Sur" and the diversion of the river to the south. The drained riverbed became a magnificent garden complex and brought verdant colour into the city. Although València is surrounded by industrial and business parks, the city has plenty to offer in the area between the coastline and old quarter – including more than 40 museums. The water quality at the beaches is usually good, and, in the early months of the year, the air is scented by orange blossom.

VALÈNCIA

Museu de Belles Arts ★

Carrer de Ruaya

Carrer de Sagunt

Carrer d'Almassor

A. de la Constitució

Carrer del Pla de la Saïdia

C. del Guadalaviar

Avinguda de Pius XII

Avinguda de Menéndez Pidal

C. de Guillem de Castro

12 Institut Valencià
d'Art Modern (IVAM)

Torres de Serrans **11**

13 Bioparc

Passeig de la Petxina

C. de Sant Miquel

C. d. C. dels Cavallers

Carrer del Doctor Zamenhof

Gran Via de Ferran el Catòlic

Carrer de Quart

Carrer de Quart

Ana Eva

Carrer de Quart

C. del Turia

C. de Guillem de Castro

C. de Lepant

C. dels Cavallers

3
Parroquia de
San Nicolás

2 Plaça de la Verge

1 Catedral ★

Llotja de la Seda ★ **4**

Mercat Central ★

5 Plaça Santa Catalina

Carrer de la Pe

Central Bar

C. de Joan Llorenç

C. de Maldonado

Avinguda de l'Oest

Carrer de
Sant Vicent Màrtir

6
El Palacio del
Marqués de Dos Aguas

7
El Patriarca

Carrer de
Pascual i Genís

Carrer de Colón

C. de Guillem de Castro

Carrer de Xàtiva

Gran Via de Ramón y Cajal

Carrer de Pelai

Gran Via del Marquè

Carrer d'Alacant

Carrer de Dénia

Carrer de Cadis

Carrer de Sant Vicent Màrtir

Carrer de les Filipines

C. del Literat Azorín

C. dels Centelles

Parc Central

Avinguda de Perís i Valero

Avinguda d'Ausiàs March

Carretera de Malilla

C. de Juan Ramón Jiménez

MARCO POLO HIGHLIGHTS

★ **CATEDRAL**
Awesome building full of art and
tradition ➤ p. 60

★ **LLOTJA/LONJA DE LA SEDA**
The magnificent Gothic Silk Exchange
bears testimony to the prosperity of
former times ➤ p. 62

★ **CIUTAT DE LES ARTS I LES CIÈNCIES**
Modern architecture that sets new
standards ➤ p. 63

★ **JARDINS/JARDINES DEL TURIA**
The city's 'green lung' grew out of the
drained bed of the River Turia ➤ p. 64

★ **MUSEU DE BELLES ARTS**
A treasure trove of art by Velázquez,
Goya, Sorolla and more. ➤ p. 64

★ **LAS FALLAS**
The spectacular festival is now
recognised by UNESCO as an example
of intangible cultural heritage ➤ p. 64

★ **MERCAT/MERCADO CENTRAL**
One of the most beautiful markets in
Spain ➤ p. 67

★ **L'ALBUFERA**
Nature in its purest form, south of the
city ➤ p. 68

VALÈNCIA

(□ E6) **Cosmopolitan atmosphere, incredible beaches and parks, grand museums and modern architecture – that's València for you (population 800,000).**

A dynamic facelift has turned València into one of Spain's most popular destinations for a city break, and its "City of the Arts and Sciences" into an international architectural landmark. The splendid Old Town and many of the promenades were spruced up; the harbour and sea-front area changed completely. This charming and vivacious Mediterranean metropolis is at its liveliest during *Las Fallas* (see p. 64) in March.

Hoping to get around without breaking the bank? Best pick up the

WHERE TO START?

The *Miguelete belltower* shows the way. Regardless of whether you arrive at the Pl. de la Reina or the Pl. de la Virgen, from here you can allow yourself to drift. Head either to the bustling centre around the town hall square (Plaça de l'Ajuntament) or stroll through the alleys of the Old Town quarter, El Carmen. Don't worry about getting lost – sooner or later you'll hit the ring road C/ Colón/Guillem de Castro or the Jardines de Turia. València is easy to explore on foot! For longer distances, use the well-maintained Metro or municipal bus network.

🐦 *València Tourist Card.* Order in advance with an online discount and then collect it from one of the tourist information offices once you're there. The card gives you discounts in museums and shops, and you can use public transport in fare zone A and the metro line to and from the airport for free. The card is just 13.50 euros for 24 hours, 18 for 48 and 22.50 for 72 hours with the online discount *(visit valencia.com).*

SIGHTSEEING

1 CATEDRAL ★

The Cathedral is a heady mix of architectural styles, ranging from Gothic to neo-Classicism. The forerunners of the mediaeval house of worship (13th century) were a Roman temple and the main mosque from the Moorish period. The *Puerta de Palau*, one of the cathedral's three porches, dates from this early period. On the exterior, the Baroque *Puerta de los Hierros* and the Gothic *Apostle Gateway* with its numerous figures are well worth seeing, especially when the *Water Court* convenes in front of the gateway every Thursday at midday to solve problems concerning water rights. Highlights in the interior include: the *Santo Cáliz Chapel* with the 'Holy Grail', the *Borgia Chapel* with Goya's masterful painting *San Francisco y el Moribundo Impenitente*, the high altar, the arm relic of Saint Vincent Martyr in the *Capilla de la Resurrección*, and the *cathedral museum*, with its exhibits of sacred art, including paintings by Vicent Macip (1475–1545), one of the

The dizzying view from the cathedral's bell tower

most important Renaissance masters in Spain and father of the no less famous painter Juan de Juanes. *(Mon–Sat 10am–6.30pm, Sun 2–6.30pm | audio guide | catedraldevalencia.es | Plaza de la Reina | ○ 30 mins).*

You should also take the time to climb up the almost 51-m-high bell tower *El Miguelete (April–Oct, daily 10am–7.30pm; otherwise Mon–Fri 10am–6.30pm, Sat 10am–7pm, Sun 10am–1pm and 5.30–7pm)* from the 14th/15th century, a work by Andrés Juliá. The tower is named after Miguel (English: Michael) because the largest bell in it was consecrated on Michaelmas Day.

2 PLAÇA/PLAZA DE LA VIRGEN

Terrace cafés and orange trees create the very special atmosphere of this square at the back of the cathedral. This was the site of the forum in Roman days. The most important building is the *Basílica de la Mare de Déu dels Desamparats*, where the picture of the "Holy Virgin of the Defenceless" is revered.

3 PARROQUIA DE SAN NICOLÁS

What they saw when they removed the plaster of the church of San Nicolás in 1958 came as a real shock to the site's researchers: the most spectacular frescoes from floor to ceiling. This find has since earned the now carefully restored church the nickname the "Sistine Chapel of València". The vast abundance of colours and images will be sure to impress even the most reluctant sightseers. *July–Sept, Tue–Fri 10.30am–9pm, Sat 10.30am–7.30pm, Sun 11.30am–9pm, slightly shorter in winter | admission 7 euros | C/ Caballeros 35 | sannicolasvalencia. com | ○ 45 mins.*

The magnificent columned hall in the Llotja de la Seda was home to the city's silk trade

◪ LLOTJA/LONJA DE LA SEDA ★

The word alone exudes a certain magic: silk. Starting in the late 15th century, merchants went about their business in València's Silk Exchange, which is now one of Unesco's World Heritage Sites. The towering building, also known as *Lonja de los Mercaderes*, has spiral columns and combines Gothic with early-Renaissance elements. The Orange Tree Patio adjoins the building. The "Sea Consulate" next door used to supervise maritime transport. The exchange was once full of tables where the wholesalers and retailers signed their contracts. With a little imagination, the columns can be interpreted as palm trees expanding at the top to support the late-Gothic arches. *Tue–Sat 10am–2pm, 3–7pm, Sun 10am–3pm | Plaza del Mercat | ⏱ 45 mins.*

◫ PLAÇA/PLAZA SANTA CATALINA

Lively inner-city square with the Baroque bell tower of the Santa Catalina Church. The cool tiger-nut milk *horchata* is stirred fresh every day in the *Horchatería El Siglo*. You can visit the Gothic *Santa Catalina Church* on the adjacent *Plaza Lope de Vega* and buy embroidery and lace on the renovated "Round Square", *Plaça/Plaza Redonda*.

INSIDER TIP
A delicious cold drink

◼ EL PALACIO DEL MARQUÉS DE DOS AGUAS

The fact that the National Ceramics Museum is housed here is beside the point for many visitors, who are more interested in seeing the former living quarters of the marquis – from the pompous extravagances to original details. The imposing alabaster entrance is also impressive. *Tue–Sat 10am–2pm and 4–8pm, Sun 10am–2pm | admission 1.50 euros, Sat afternoon and Sun free admission | C/ del Poeta Querol 2 | mnceramica.mcu.es|* ⏱ *30 mins.*

7 EL PATRIARCA

València's most beautiful Renaissance church simply overflows with an abundance of decoration. A very special atmosphere is created with the Gregorian chants sung by a 20-member choir on Thursday evening at 6.30pm and Tue–Sun during Lauds at 9.30am. The choral tradition dates back to the year *1604*. *C/ de la Nau 1| patriarcavalencia.es*

veet singing n the choir

8 CIUTAT DE LES ARTS I LES CIÈNCIES ★ ⛱

Dazzling white buildings, inlaid broken tiles, monumental sculptural forms: the modern "City of the Arts and Sciences", which combines the fascinating architectural concepts of Santiago Calatrava and Félix Candela, offers both culture and leisure activities. The series of buildings in the complex were all opened in the years between 1998 and 2009 and include the *Palau de les Arts Reina Sofía* (concert hall and opera house), the *Hemisfèric* (Imax cinema), which resembles a gigantic eye, the *Umbracle* (the verdant "foyer" of the complex), the *Ágora* events and art hall, the *Museu de les Ciències Príncipe Felipe* (science museum,

open daily in summer 10am–9pm and in the winter Mon–Thu 10am–6pm, Fri–Sun 10am–7pm) and the Oceanogràfic aquarium (Sun–Fri 10am–6pm, Sat 10am–8pm, slight variations in early and late summer 10am–7pm/8pm, mid-July–end of Aug daily 10am–midnight). Santiago Calatrava's architectural contribution is the *Pont L'Assut d'Or*, a steel-and-concrete bridge whose piers rise up 123m and are connected by steel cables arranged in the shape of a harp.

The complex isn't just meant to be admired from a distance. The 900-m² screen in the *Hemisfèric* (3-D projections, daily changing programmes, generally 10am–8pm) draws the audience into the action. Similarly, the exhibits in the Science Museum are designed to be touched and explored. Children will have a lot of fun with the *Espai dels Xiquets* and "Exploratorium". A sculpture measuring 15m visualises the genetic fingerprint, a gigantic Foucault's Pendulum demonstrates the rotation of the earth.

The highlight of the excellently planned *Oceanogràfic* is the underwater glass tunnel in the "Oceans" section, where sharks and rays float above the heads of the visitors. There are white whales in the "Arctic" section, penguins in the "Antarctic" and regular dolphin shows in the *Delfinario*.

You will be able to save money if you buy the 🦐 three-way combined ticket (ask for *conjunta*) for the Hemisfèric, Science Museum and Oceanogràfic. *Av. del Professor López Piñero 3–7 | cac.es*

9 JARDINS/JARDINES DEL TURIA ★

Until recently, València was somewhat of a "Cinderella" among the cities on Spain's southeast coast. But in just the past two decades, the city has undergone a total makeover. After the catastrophic flood of 1957, the River Turia was widely diverted to the south, far away from the city, and the dried out riverbed was then used to create large new gardens and parks. Today, there are countless palms and orange trees, as well as fountains and even football grounds. The city's inhabitants have become very fond of the 7.5-km strip of green that runs through the city all the way to the *Ciutat de les Arts i les Ciències*.

10 MUSEU DE BELLES ARTS ★ ☂

Art lovers will delight in the *Museu de Belles Arts*, València's fine art gallery. The scope of the exhibits in the museum ranges from Roman objects and magnificent altar paintings to 20th-century artworks. There are works by all of the famous names in Spanish painting, including Diego de Velázquez, Alonso Cano, Juan Ribalta, Francisco de Goya and Joaquín Sorolla, in addition to an interesting choice of temporary exhibitions. The building dates back to the 17th century when it was an educational establishment for young people who would later play a role in the church. The museum's café-restaurant is also a nice place to relax. *Tue–Sun 10am–8pm | free*

FIRE, FIRE!

València throws restraint to the wind every March during ★ ⚑ *Las Fallas* (fallasvalencia.es) – a mega festival. On 15/16 of the month, colossal effigies and entire ensembles of figures, the so-called *plantà*, are erected everywhere in the city. The gigantic sculptures are real works of art and can be compared with the floats that feature in large carnival processions in other countries. The basic materials are usually wood and papier-mâché; the costs sometimes exceed 200,000 euros for a single unit!

The topics range from satirically distorted effigies of politicians to caricatures of the country's football gods, models and other stars – in fact, anyone that *Valencianos* think need to be brought down a peg or two. But these artificial figures *(ninots)* only have a short lifespan. The sometimes house-high sculptures are eventually subjected to flaming scorn in its full sense. On the Night of Fire *(nit de foc*, 18/19 March), a gigantic fireworks display is organised. Then, from 19 to 20 March, the figures are burnt in the *Cremá*, accompanied by numerous gun salutes, fireworks and – to be on the safe side – the fire brigade. If you miss *Las Fallas*, you can always explore some of the most beautiful *ninots* from years gone by in the *Museo Fallero (Mon–Sat 10am–7pm, Sun 10am–2pm | admission 2 euros | Pl. de Monteolivete 4)*.

Joggers appreciate the shade in the Jardins del Turia

admission | C/ San Pio V 9 | museo bellasartesvalencia.gva.es | ⊙ 1 hour

⑪ TORRES DE SERRANS/ SERRANOS

If you're going to climb one high building during your València visit, make it this impressive city gate. Numerous staircases and intermediate levels eventually reveal a panorama over the Old Town and the riverbed of the Turia Gardens. We promise it's worth the effort! The towers were built as part of the city walls at the end of the 14th century and are today one of the city's landmarks. *Mon–Sat 9.30am–7pm (in winter until 6pm), Sun 10am–2pm| admission free* | ⊙ 30 mins

⑫ INSTITUT VALENCIÀ D'ART MODERN (IVAM)

Temporary exhibitions of works by contemporary artists are held in the modern main building of the Institute for Modern Art. The IVAM has an enormous art collection and regularly exchanges works with museums from all over the world. A permanent exhibition is devoted to the oeuvre of the sculptor Julio González (1876–1942). The Hall of the Great Wall *(Sala de la Muralla)*, in which a section of the mediaeval city wall runs between modern columns, is unusual and makes a particularly interesting setting for exhibitions. *Tue–Sun 10am–7pm (Fri until 9pm)| Sun free admission | Guillem de Castro 118 | ivam.es/en*

⑬ BIOPARC 🐵

A little piece of African savannah, complete with wild animals, at the heart of the big city – that is what the *Bioparc* offers. The complex is located

Mercat Central

in the *Parque de Cabecera*, an extension of the *Jardines del Turia* park. Rhinoceroses, lions, giraffes, elephants, lemurs and monkeys are just some of the animals you can see. *Daily in summer 10.30am–7.30pm, in winter 10am–7pm | admission 23.80 euros, children (4–12 years) 18 euros, under 4 years free | Av. Pío Baroja 3 | bioparcvalencia.es | ⏱ 1½ hrs*

EATING & DRINKING

ANA EVA
This vegetarian restaurant can be found between the Quart Towers and the Botanical Garden. It serves organic food, sometimes with an exotic twist. The interior is simple, but friendly. Only open *Thu–Sun | C/ Turia 49 | tel. 9 63 91 53 69 | restaurante anaeva.es | €–€€*

> **INSIDER TIP** Organic options

CASA CARMELA ⚑
Famous for cooking up shockingly good paella, this restaurant is located on La Malva-Rosa beach with no fewer than 20 different options cooked over a wood fire daily. *Open daily, lunchtime only | C/ Isabel de Villena 155 | tel. 9 63 71 00 73 | casacarmela.com | €€*

CENTRAL BAR
Star chef Ricard Camarena is a true master of modern cuisine. Thankfully, anyone can afford to sample the tapas at his bar in the market hall. *Tue–Sat 8.30am–3.30pm | Pl. del Mercat | ricardcamarena.com | €–€€*

RIFF
Originally from the Black Forest in Germany, Chef Bernd Knöller (one Michelin star) goes all out for his guests. He has lived in Spain for years and creates genuine works of art inspired by the freshness of Mediterranean cuisine. There's a wonderful selection of more than 200 wines to choose from. *Thu–Sat 1.30–3.30pm, 9–10.30pm, closed Sun–Wed | C/ Conde Altea 18 | tel. 9 63 33 53 53 | restaurante-riff.com | €€€*

SHOPPING

The experts have still not made up their minds. Is Barcelona's *Boquería* or

València's ★ ☂ *Mercat Central* *(Mercado Central | Mon–Sat 7am–3pm | Plaza del Mercat 6 | mercadocentral valencia.es)* the most beautiful market in Spain? The art nouveau building covers 8,000m² and is groaning with stalls selling sausages, fruit, vegetables, fish and meat. This is where most of the locals prefer to shop – also for cheese, spices, fig marmalade and tomato conserves. Whether you buy anything or not, a visit is always an experience.

Another historical building, the *Mercat Colón* (Mercado Colón) on C/ Jorge Juan, lies at the heart of an upscale shopping area where you will find many exclusive shoe shops. The C/ de las Cestas is famous for its handcrafted goods made of willow basketwork. In the Barri del Carmen around the C/ Bolsería, C/ Quart and Pl. del Tossal, you will find unusual fashion shops.

There are several branches of the *El Corte Inglés* department store chain on C/ Pintor Sorolla 26, C/ Pintor Maella 37, C/ Menéndez Pidal 15 and C/ Colón 27. For vibrant markets selling all kinds of wares *(mercadillos)* head to the *Mercadillo Jerusalén-Pelayo (Convento Jerusalén | Gran Vía Ramón y Cajal)* on Tuesdays and to the *Mercadillo Mosén Sorell (Plaza Mossén Sorell)* on Wednesdays.

BEACHES

València has more than 7km of beaches. The best section starts north of the port where you'll find the adjoining *Las Arenas* and *Malvarossa* beaches; they are lined with beautiful promenades.

SPORT & ACTIVITIES

Visitors who like jogging, cycling or just going for a walk will find just what they are looking for right at the heart of the city in the *Jardines del Turia* and along the beachside promenades. Register with *Valencia Bikes (C/ Tapinería 14 | tel. 6 50 62 14 36 | valenciabikes.com)* in order to join one of their excellent guided English-language cycle tours for a minimum of two participants; they also provide the bikes. For those who prefer to be independent, it is also possible to hire bikes for your own individual sightseeing tour.

INSIDER TIP
Rollin', rollin', rollin'

TOMATO FIGHT

Strictly speaking, this strange event in late August in the small town of Buñol, west of València, no longer passes for an insider tip – after all, the Chinese, Korean, Japanese and American press cover it every year. Still, if you're ever in the market for a truly unique experience, the *tomatina* tomato fight is the perfect place for you. Join thousands of crazy revellers as they dive into truckloads of overripe tomatoes. Make sure you wear old clothes, protect your camera… and then jump in! *latomatina.info*

NIGHTLIFE

The traditional nightlife scene in València is focused on the Old Town district *Barri del Carmen*. A popular nightlife zone, particularly for alternative venues, is *Ruzafa*, where you'll find tapas bars, jazz venues, rock venues and much more besides. Students prefer to meet up between the Av. de Aragón and the Pl. del Cedro. Anyone searching for smarter options should look in the direction of the Marina and the *Marina Beach Club (marinabeachclub.com)*. For something a little more colourful, head to *Radio City (C/ Santa Teresa 19 | radiocityvalencia.es)* which hosts DJ sessions and live flamenco. The *Palau de la Música* offers a wide range of concerts from classical and jazz to pop *(Paseo de la Alameda 30 | tel. 9 63 37 50 20 | palaudevalencia.com)*.

INSIDER TIP
The night is long

AROUND VALÈNCIA

L'ALBUFERA ★

25km / 40 mins by car via the CV-500

Vietnam, in the middle of Spain? No need to jet off to Asia for rice fields as far as the eye can see – just take the number 25 bus and head to the south of the city. That's where the *Parque Natural de l'Albufera* begins, with its rice fields, pine forests and beach dunes. The nature reserve is named after the wide Albufera Lake, and its fresh water doesn't just feed the rice fields. It is also home to a vast bird sanctuary with countless ducks, moorhens and herons. Once a small island hamlet surrounded by water, the small village of El Palmar is now mainly a paella-on-Sunday destination for *Valèncianos* and the starting point for boat tours *(paseos en barca)*.

Ducks, herons and rare ibis rule the roost in the Albufera nature reserve

t's a stunningly romantic spot, especially in the evening when the sun sets behind the lagoon. If you don't fancy the regular bus, the *Bus Turístic (valenciabusturistic.com)* also goes here. 🚌 E6-7

SAGUNT (SAGUNTO)
39km / 30 mins by car via the V-31
Get up close and personal with Ancient Rome. Sagunt, a town (pop. 66,000) north of València, has a history going back more than 2,000 years, as seen in the *Teatre Romà (Tue–Sat 10am– 8pm, in winter to 6pm, Sun 10am–2pm)*. The complex as we see it today has been extensively renovated, but in Roman times the theatre could accommodate an audience of 4,000. The path up to the castle *(Tue–Sat 10am-8pm, in winter to 6pm, Sun 10am–2pm)* from the theatre is lined with cactuses and pine trees. You can delve deeply into the Roman past in the *Museo Histórico (C/ Castillo 24 | Tue–Sat 10am-8pm,*

in winter to 6pm, Sun 10am–2pm | 🕐 *1 hour)*. Sgunt also honours the *Fallas* tradition in March. 🚌 E5

CULLERA
47km / 45 mins by car via the V-41 and the A-38
This pleasant seaside destination (pop.24,000) south of València is popular with city dwellers in search of relaxation. The *castle*, which the Christians conquered from the Moors in 1239, towers over the Old Town. The water park *Aquópolis (mid-July–early Sept, daily 12-7pm, otherwise 12–6pm | admission 26.95 euros, children from 90-140cm 20.95 euros, children under 90cm go free | Ctra. Nazaret-Oliva | cullera.aquopolis.es)* is open during the summer months. The water park boasts the "Minipark" for the little ones and "Black Hole" and "Kamikaze" for braver teens. 🚌 F7

XÀTIVA (JÁTIVA)
63km / 55 mins by car via the A-7
Xàtiva/Játiva (pop. 30,000), to the south of València, is surrounded by orange groves and hills. There are two castles on the rocky massif above the pleasant little town; the walls of the *Castillo Mayor* and *Castillo Menor* spread picturesquely across the top of the hills. Mention should also be made of the *Santa María* collegiate church and the memorial to two of the small town's most famous sons: the Popes Calisto III (1378-1458) and Alexander VI (1431-1503); both members of the infamous Borgia family. The highlight of the year is the *feria* in August. 🚌 E7–8

COSTA BLANCA

SUN, SEA & HINTERLAND

The Costa Blanca, the "White Coast", boasts the ABC of Spanish holidays: A for Alicante, B for Benidorm and C for Calp. A number of other towns also have perfect beaches and have received the coveted Blue Flag for their cleanliness time and again.

But that's not all. The beautiful hinterland has so much to offer from quaint little villages to lonely hiking trails, magical stalactite caves and mysterious rock formations. The summer season brings

Blue sky, turquoise sea and white sand at Cap de la Nao, Xàbia

hustle and bustle to the coast and the inevitable battles to secure the best spot for your towel at the beach, not to mention at the hotel pool! But by September, you'll have the beaches and promenades almost to yourself. And some people who once visited the Costa Blanca as guests from northern Europe end up making the coast their new home – not least because it promises more than 300 days of sunshine a year.

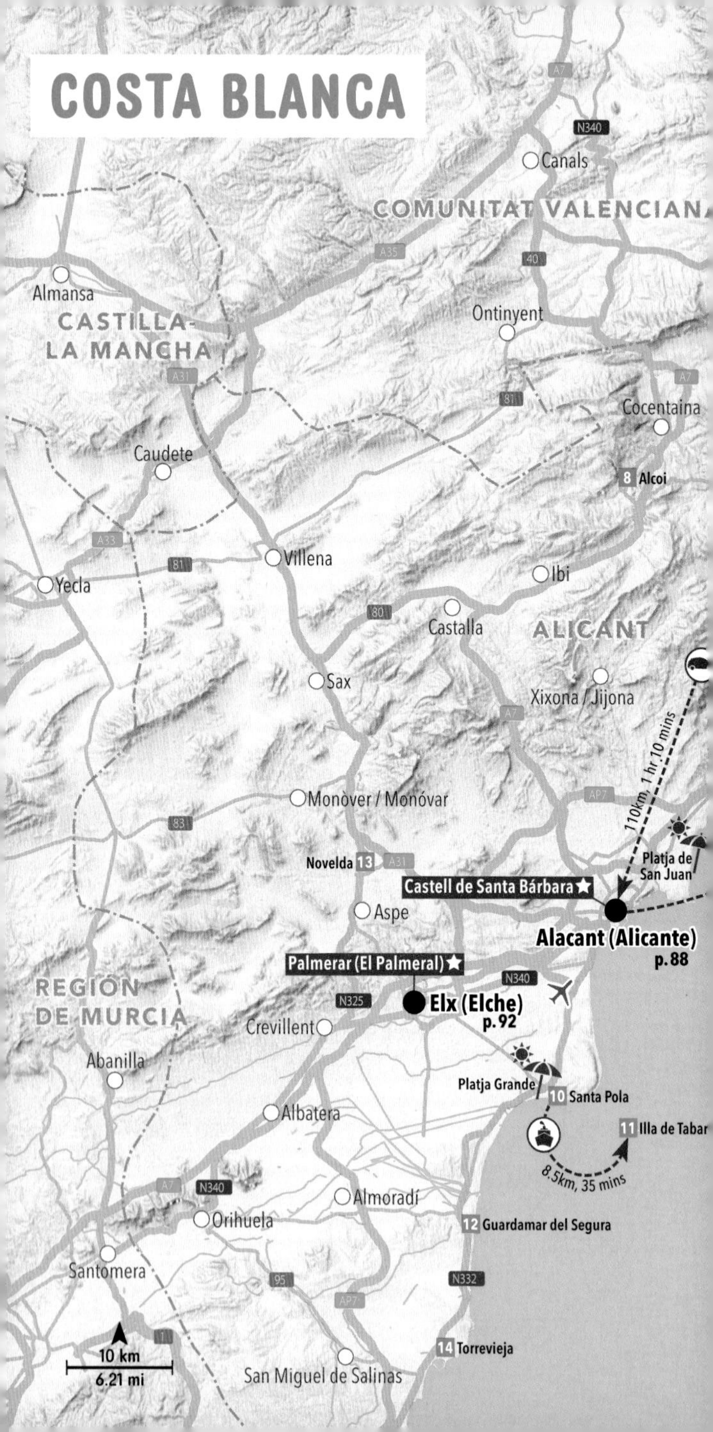

COSTA BLANCA
A7
N340
Canals
COMUNITAT VALENCIANA
A35
40
Almansa
CASTILLA-LA MANCHA
Ontinyent
A31
81
A7
Cocentaina
Caudete
8 Alcoi
A33
Villena
81
Ibi
Yecla
80
Castalla
ALICANT
Sax
Xixona / Jijona
A7
110km, 1 hr 10 mins
AP7
Monòver / Monóvar
83
Platja de San Juan
Novelda 13
A31
Castell de Santa Bárbara
Aspe
Alacant (Alicante) p. 88
Palmerar (El Palmeral)
N340
REGIÓN DE MURCIA
N325
Elx (Elche) p. 92
Crevillent
Abanilla
Platja Grande
10 Santa Pola
Albatera
11 Illa de Tabarca
8.5km, 35 mins
A7
N340
Almoradí
Orihuela
12 Guardamar del Segura
Santomera
95
N332
AP7
14 Torrevieja
10 km
6.21 mi
San Miguel de Salinas

Platja de Gandía

1 Gandia

○ Oliva

○ Pego

Dénia
p. 74

Cova de les Calaveres **2**

Xàbia (Jávea) **3**
Platja de l'Arenal

Benissa

4 Moraira

7
Guadalest ★

6
Fonts de l'Algar
(Fuentes del Algar)

Calp (Calpe)
p. 77

Penyal d'Ifac (Peñón de Ifach) ★

Altea **5**

○ l'Alfàs del Pi

Platja de Ponent
Platja de Llevant

51km, 35 mins

Benidorm
p. 80

9
Vila Joiosa
(Villajoyosa)

45km, 30 mins

MAR

MEDITERRÁNEO

DÉNIA

(🗺 F-G8) **The gateway (ferry port) to the Balearic Islands and an important port, Dénia (pop. 42,000) has retained its maritime character.**

The area around Dénia is relatively densely settled, but fortunately there are fewer high-rise buildings than on many other sections of the coast. The areas you should visit are clearly defined; the broad harbour front and the castle. It is always fun to watch the fishing boats return to port – you can witness the spectacle between 3.30pm and 6pm on weekdays. And because of all the fresh fish here,

some particularly good restaurants have made Dénia their home.

CASTELL

Let's go! Or more precisely, *up* we go! The path up to the walls and castle starts behind the arcaded front of the town hall and you will soon see a Moorish archway. The *Torre Islámica*, a well-preserved watchtower, which can be reached along a path leading through a lovely pine grove, is another indication of Moorish presence. From here, you will have your first good view of the Montgó Massif. You might be out of breath when you finally

As night falls, the restaurant tables in Dénia's old town fill up with diners

reach the top plateau with the *Palau del Gobernador* and *Museu Arqueològic*, the entrance fee includes admission to the small archaeological museum. Concerts are occasionally held in the castle in summer. It is especially atmospheric to visit the illuminated site at night – in July and August the castle is sometimes open until after midnight. *July–mid-Sept daily 10am–8.30pm and on some days until 00.30am, shorter opening hours for the rest of the year | admission 3 euros, children under 16 1 euro | denia.net | ⏱ 2 hours.*

MUSEU DELS JOGUETS

Ah, to be a child again… Toy museum with doll's houses and cars from times gone by let you indulge in nostalgia for an hour or so. Entrance free. *Daily 10am–1pm, 4–8pm (in summer 5–9pm) | C/ Calderón | ⏱ 45 mins.*

EATING & DRINKING

MENA ⚑

What a restaurant, and what a view! This restaurant overlooking the coast near Platja Arenetes offers dishes ranging from sea bass to platters of grilled fish. There are also special meals for children. *Daily 10.30am–1pm, Sun until 7.30pm | Ctra. Las Rotas, km 5 | tel. 9 65 78 09 43 | restaurantemena.es | €€*

QUIQUE DACOSTA

Hoping to treat yourself? How does a 7-course menu sound? This gourmet restaurant from the chef of the same name has three Michelin stars. But make sure to book in well in advance! *Open daily 1.30–2.30pm, 8.30–9.30pm for food and until 1am for drinks | C/ Rascassa 1 | tel. 9 65 78 41 79 | quiquedacosta.es | €€€*

SHOPPING

The *weekly market (Mon–Sat 9am–3pm)* offers a wide range of regional organic products. The stalls are housed inside the busy market hall but also spill outside onto C/ Magallanes. Things also get quite lively in the C/ Marqués de Campo and the C/ Loreto. A *mercadillo (8am–1.30pm)* is held on the *Explanada Torrecremada* on Monday morning as is a *rastro de antigüedades* (flea and antiques market) on Friday morning. In summer, there is a *mercadillo (6pm until midnight and until 1am on weekends)* every evening on the *Explanada Cervantes*, with colourful stalls selling costume jewellery, paintings, leather goods and other handicrafts.

BEACHES

The small town of Dénia boasts around 20km of coastline separated into the northern *(Área Les Marines)* and southern beaches *(Playas de las Rotas)* by the port. While the "northern beaches" score top marks for their wide expanses of yellow sand, the "southern beaches" offer a string of smaller, rather stony, coves. The only exception is the sandy *Platja Marineta Cassiana* near the port.

SPORT & ACTIVITIES

INSIDER TIP
Beach route

One of the most beautiful ways to keep fit is simply to walk or jog for miles along the beautiful seashore, past the *Platja Marineta Cassiana* and *Platja El Trampoli* and as far as the *Punta Negra*; the route includes the tarmacked promenade, but also dirt paths and small side roads, all of which are well suited for jogging.

Boat trips are available at the harbour, e.g. by *Mundo Marino (Av. Juan Fuster 2 | tel. 9 66 42 30 66 | mundomarino.es)* on various routes along the coast.

A popular hiking destination, the *Parc Natural Montgó*, can be found in the hinterland of Dénia. The local tourist office *(Plaza Oculista Biges | tel. 9 66 42 33 67 | denia.net)* and the Centro de Interpretatión *(Finca Bosc de Diana | Camí Sant Joan 1 | tel. 9 66 46 71 55)* can provide further information. You can choose between several hiking trails starting from the entrance at *Camí del Pou de la Montaña*; these include one to the *Cova de l'Aigua* (1.6km), one to the *Racó del Bou* (2.6km) and another up to the 753-m-high peak *Creueta* (8.5km).

NIGHTLIFE

The trendiest place to go out at night is on the south side of the marina *Escullera Sud*; the area around C/ La Mar is also quite popular. *Zensa Marina (Puerto Deportivo Marina de Dénia | C/ Darsena de Vapor | zensamarina.zensa.es)* is a popular disco with lounge and cool pool parties.

AROUND DÉNIA

🚩 GANDIA (GANDÍA)
36km / 35 mins by car via the AP-7

Located to the north-west of Dénia, the city (pop. 75,000) is a must for anyone interested in history or who has heard of the Borgia popes. Few clans can claim to be as power-hungry or corrupt as that of Pope Alexander VI in Rome around 1500. The 🎯 *Palau Ducal dels Borja (Tue–Sat 10am–2pm and 4–8pm, Sun 10am–2pm | admission 7 euros | C/ Duc Alfons el Vell 1 | palauducal.com | ⏱ 45 mins)* is where the family lived before moving to the Vatican. Gandía's beautiful sandy beach, the 🏖 *Platja de Gandía*, is famous nationwide as a holiday destination. *⃞ F8*

🚩 COVA DE LES CALAVERES (CUEVA DE LAS CALAVERAS) 🎯
16km / 20 mins by car via the CV-725 and the CV-731

The name, "Skull Cave", isn't exactly inviting, especially for holidaymakers and it's also a little misleading since you won't find any bones in the cave today. The cave is also known as *Cova de Benidoleig* (remember this for signposting) and once provided shelter for prehistoric people, but the bones that were found here date from

The coast around Xàbia features rocky promontories and cliff-backed coves

the Islamic period; it is assumed that some peoplpe became trapped inside the cave while they were looking for water. The story about a Moorish prince who supposedly tried to hide from El Cid in the cave with 150 members of his harem can probably be relegated to the realm of legend. *Daily, in summer 9am–8pm, at other times 9am–6pm | cuevadelascalaveras.com |* 🕑 *30 mins | ▥ F8*

❸ XÀBIA (JÁVEA)

11km / 20 mins by car via the CV-736
This pleasant town (pop. 27,000) extends along the coast and can boast some beautiful beaches; at the top of the list is ✹ *Platja de l'Arenal* where visitors will find plenty of places to stop for refreshments. The *Parador (Av. del Mediterráneo | parador.es | €€€)*, a four-star hotel surrounded by a grove of palm trees, is at the other end of the

promenade. The harbour spreads out below Cap Sant Antoni, and a second promontory juts out into the sea south-east of Xàbia: *Cap de la Nao (or Nau)*. A lighthouse rises up above the cape, and there are wonderful panoramic views of the rocky coast. *▥ G8*

CALP (CALPE)

(▥ F9) **The town and its rocky massif are certainly eye-catching – the soaring Penyal d'Ifac/Peñón de Ifach is one of the symbols of the Mediterranean coast.**

Early Phoenician mariners admired the 332-m-high limestone rock that rises up behind Calp and called it the "Rock of the North". At the base of the rock – probably the most photographed on the coast – is a small seaside town and port (pop. 23,000) that was once a fishing village. In 1238, the Christians took Calp back from the Moors and soon afterwards started exploiting the salt in the area. In 1744, in an attack, they drove back 800 pirates. In recent years, many people from other parts of Europe have settled in the area and a blanket of houses now reaches far up into the hills. The salt works are of historical importance, and there are examples of significant modern architecture by Ricardo Bofill: *La Muralla Roja*, *El Anfitteatro* and *Xanadú*.

SIGHTSEEING

OLD TOWN

Calp's Old Town is mainly visible in the area around the Plaza de la Vila, in the remains of the city wall, the Gothic Mudéjar-style church (15th century),

the modern church *Virgen de las Nieves* and the *Collectors' Museum* containing changing exhibitions (*Museo del Coleccionismo* | *Tue–Sat 10am–2pm, 4.30–7.30pm* | *admission free* | *Plaça de la Villa 15*).

HARBOUR

The lively sport and fishing harbour brings together elegant yachts and local fishermen mending their nets. Many restaurants focus on seafood: the fish auction takes place at around 4pm or 5pm from Monday to Friday and is dominated by the shouts of traders, accompanied by the screeching of the seagulls outside.

INSIDER TIP
Going once going twic

PENYAL D'IFAC (PEÑÓN DE IFACH) ★

Calp's gigantic cliff, a favourite photo

The Calp coastline is especially beautiful when viewed from the sea

motif for millions of visitors to the Costa Blanca, is protected as a *National Park*, providing a home for numerous types of seabirds and plants. The *Passeig Ecològic Principe de Asturias*, a well-maintained path, curves its way around the west and south precipices behind the harbour. Overshadowed by the massive Peñón, it continues past the stony *El Racó* Bay and opens up wonderful views of the coast and mountains. The hike up the Ifach itself is one of the single most extraordinary on the Costa Blanca. The fortress-like rock towers 332m above the sea like a "Little Gibraltar", only with an even better view. Few other places along the coast can claim such a prominent mix of the natural and man-made. On one side: the shining blue of the Mediterranean, fragrant plants and the shrieks of seagulls. On the other: the high-rise blocks of Calpe, towering on the horizon like a strange man-made mirage.

EATING & DRINKING

LAS BARCAS

Enjoy the atmosphere of the port with the daily set menu or one of the many varieties of paella. Nice terrace. *Open daily | Explanada del Puerto 14 | tel. 9 65 83 85 93 | €–€€*

LA CASA

Excellent food – especially the steaks. Due to limited capacity, it is advisable to book a table. *Wed–Sat 7–11pm, Sun 12–4pm, closed Jan.–March | C/ del Mar 23 | tel. 9658373 12 | €€*

BEACHES

Calp's beaches and coves are located on both sides of the *Peñón de Ifach*. To the west these include the small *Playa Cantal-Roig*, the *Cala Morelló* and the 1.2-km-long *Playa Arenal-Bol* with a nice promenade. North of Peñon de Ifach there is the 950-m-long strip of sand that makes up the *Playa de Levante* (also: *Playa La Fossa*).

In summer, a variety of boat tours, both along the coast and to Altea and Benidorm, depart from the port. You can hire bicycles from *Sol y Bike (C/ Blasco Ibañez 10-A | tel. 6 76 86 74 45 | solybike. com). Las Antípodas (Ctra. Calpe–Moraira, km 2 | tel. 6 65 85 32 00 | lasantipodas.com)* organises many water-sports activities such as sailing, sea kayaking, wakeboarding and stand-up paddling.

NIGHTLIFE

There's always something going on in the bars and pubs around C/ La Niña, e.g. in *Déjà vu*. If you want to get your dancing shoes on, head to *Camaleón* disco *(C/ Gibraltar | Edificio Voramar)*.

AROUND CALP

🔳 MORAIRA

14km / 25 mins by car via the CV-746 coastal road

A densely settled stretch of coast with many bays, and coastline shared by

villas and pine trees, separates Calp from Moraira (pop. 14,500). The bulky round tower of the *castle* (18th century) between the *Platja de l'Ampolla* and port presents a distinctive landmark, while the bay of Portet is known for its beautifully clear water. Cala Moraig, just a few minutes by northeast of Moraira by car, is a swimmer's paradise: rocks up to 100m high tower around the stone beach, and turquoise waves lap against the shore.
🚗 G8

INSIDER TIP
This bay is a stunner

BENIDORM

(🚗 F9) **It's hard to imagine, but as late as the 1950s, Benidorm (pop. now 72,000) was home to just 3,000 people who made a living from fishing and farming. Shortly after, mass tourism set in, leaving its mark on Benidorm with mile after mile of high-rise castles, earning the city the nickname "Manhattan on the Mediterranean".**

Today, the city's name has become a synonym for uninhibited leisure and holiday fun. Some even call it the "meat factory" due to the thousands of people crammed in like sardines on the two beaches: *Platja de Llevant (Playa Levante)* and *Platja de Ponent (Playa Poniente)*.

Platja de Levant is a prime example of what we think of as a stereotypical Spanish holiday destination, where Spaniards are outnumbered by northern Europeans for around eleven months of the year. However, come August, avalanches of cars thunder down from Madrid, heading straight

Benidorm's glittering skyline lights up the night

or Benidorm. Large Spanish families descend on the city and make themselves at home on the beach with ortilla sandwiches and Cruzcampo beer. Benidorm is certainly a bit of a numbers game: the statistics list more han 1,000 bars, restaurants and night clubs, although the exact figure isn't clear. But while this isn't suitable for those seeking peace and quiet, if you're in the mood for non-stop entertainment at the height of summer, then you've come to the right place. Thankfully, Benidorm is much quieter outside the high season; from September to May the waves tumble in on less-crowded city beaches.

SIGHTSEEING

OLD TOWN

Hard to believe, but some beautiful corners have survived in the old town

among the countless faceless highrises. Benidorm's historical origins – the settlement dates from the 14th century – are restricted to a relatively small area between the port and Playa de Levante. The name of a square is the only thing that recalls the late mediaeval castle from which the local population defended themselves against pirates from North Africa: *Plaza del Castell* – that and a few recently excavated remains of the city wall. The most important building is the *Sant Jaume* Church built in the 18th century on Plaza Sant Jaume. A statue of the patron saint the Virgen del Sufragio is honoured in the church: it is said that the wondrous sculpture of the Virgin Mary was discovered in 1740 on board an unmanned ship drifting off the coast and that it even survived a fire.

For one of the best views of the entire coast, head to the *Balcón del Mediterráneo*, just a few steps down from the Plaza del Castell. The view spans the 2km-long sandy beaches of Levant and Ponent, the 300-plus highrise towers and, yes, although it's easy to forget with all that concrete, the Mediterranean Sea.

EATING & DRINKING

The food… Well, you know those incredible Spanish bars? *Bocadillo de tortilla*, ceilings with hanging hams, greasy churros… Yeah, there's none of that. It might be an exaggeration to say that the pickle on your Big Mac is the only vegetable for miles around, but the city is not exactly a haven of

Thrill-seekers can get their kicks at Terra Mítica

culinary excellence. Luckily, there are some impressive exceptions, and the odd passable tapas bars on C/ de Santo Domingo and the neighbouring streets in the pedestrian precinct, as well as on C/ Martínez Oriola.

CLUB NÁUTICO

A pleasant place to dine near the marina away from the hustle and bustle of the city, but you can see part of Benidorm's skyline through the large windows. Freshly caught fish are sold by weight (the menu lists the price per 100g). *Daily | Paseo de Colón 2 | Puerto | tel. 9 65 85 54 25 | €€€*

ULÍA

Sophisticated dining on the beach promenade behind the Playa de Poniente. Specialities are fish and paella, including squid, rice with lobster, seafood paella, paella with rabbit.

Closed Sun evening and Mon | Av Vicente Llorca Alos 15 | near the corne of C/ Vigo | tel. 9 65 85 68 28 | €€

SHOPPING

While chains like *Zara (C/ Gambo 9, and Mango (multiple stores, including on Av. Mediterráneo 1)* have now settled in Benidorm and there's ever an outlet of the *El Corte Inglés (C Alacant 1, directly on the AP-7)* depart ment store, you don't go to Benidorm for the shopping – good boutiques here are few and far between. Instead there's a whole lot of cheap tat, bu that too can have its charms. The Chinese shops especially sell swim ming trunks and sun hats but also trashy souvenirs that are original in their own way. Why not just let your self drift around the *Plaça de la Creu.*

BEACHES

The uncontested queens among the many ★ beaches are the 🏖️ 🚩 *Platja de Llevant (Playa de Levant)* (East Beach; 2.1km long) and 🏖️ 🚩 *Platja de Ponent (Playa de Poniente)* (West Beach; 3.1km long). The two are separated by a promontory *(Balcón del Mediterráneo)* with the Old Town behind it. The port adjoins the Platja de Ponente with the 120m-long *Mal Pas Beach* near it. Two small bays behind the Platja de Levant, the *Cala Almadrava* and *Cala del Ti Ximo*, display their rugged charm. Another rocky promontory separates the Platja de Ponent from the *Cala de Finestrat*, a lovely sandy bay that belongs to the municipality of Finestrat, located 8km inland.

SPORT & ACTIVITIES

Nowhere else on the Costa Blanca offers quite as much in terms of leisure pursuits as Benidorm. Excursion boats set sail from the port in Benidorm to the *Isla de Benidorm*, *Altea*, *Calp* and the island of *Tabarca* *(e.g. Excursiones Marítimas | Passeig de Colón | tel. 9 65 85 68 87 | emb2000.es)*. Also on offer are bike rentals, kayak and diving tours, jeep safaris and paintball *(e.g. through Marco Polo Expediciones | Av. Europa 5 | tel. 9 65 86 33 99 | marcopolo-exp. es)*. A tip for golfers: the nine-hole course *Las Rejas Open Club Benidorm (C/ Presidente Adolfo Suárez 5 | tel. 9 66 88 97 75 | lasrejasbenidorm. openclub.com/)* is situated in the town,

while a little outside Is the huge *Villaitana* golf club with two 18-hole golf courses, four- and five-star hotel, a range of restaurants and swimming pools *(Av. Alcalde Eduardo Zaplana 7 | tel. 9 66 81 30 13 | meliavillaitana golf.com)*.

There are also several amusement parks in or near Benidorm. The 🎢 *Terra Mítica (mid-April-Feb, Nov, changing opening hours depending on the month and day of the week, core hours 10.30am-8pm, in high season until 10.30pm | day ticket 39 euros, children (4-12) 28 euros, cheaper online | Partida del Moralet | well-signposted | terramiticapark.com)* is home to wild rides such as the "Flight of the Phoenix" and the "Minotaur's Labyrinth". Sister park 🎢 *Terra Natura (March-Oct. daily, 10am-5/6/7/8pm depending on the month, Nov-Feb mostly just Fri-Sun 10am-5pm | admission 30, children (4-12) 25 euros, | Foia del Verdader 1 | Benidorm | terranatura.com)*

THE FESTIVAL IN THE MOUNTAINS

What a stage! Every August, the church square of the small mountain village of Polop (15km from Benidorm) hosts 🐷 *Jazzpolop*, a free jazz festival that attracts not only Spain's finest musicians, but visitors from all over the world. Meanwhile, stalls offer wine, beer and local delicacies. Plus, the show is never over before 2am! *Facebook: jazzpolop*

meanwhile gives kids the chance to get up close and personal with more than 1,500 animals, including elephants, rhinos and big cats.

Fun in the water is guaranteed at the 🐾 Aqualandia (late May–late Sept. daily 10am–7pm | aqualandia.net) water park. For an animal park complete with lemurs, penguins, flamingos and more, try 🐾 Mundomar (mid-March–Oct. daily. 10am–6pm, or in some seasons until 7/8pm | admission 30, children (3-12) 25 euros | C/ Sierra Helada | Rincón de Loix | mundomar.es). Main attractions include shows with sea lions, dolphins and parrots, plus feeding times and, rather unfortunately at somewhat high prices, activities like "swim with sea lions" and "meet the dolphins".

ENTERTAINMENT

Stories of Benidorm's nightlife have travelled far beyond the country's borders. Nightclub after nightclub is lined up along the road leading out of town towards Altea (at the exit just off the N-332) – the names surely familiar to many: Penelope (Av. Comunitat Valenciana 120km | penelopebenidorm.com), KU (Av. Comunitat Valenciana 121km | kubenidorm.es), Privilege (Av. Comunitat Valenciana 121km), Fun Factory (Av. Comunitat Valenciana 121km) and Space Morning Club (Av. Comunitat Valenciana 122km).

While it's not such a favourite with the locals, the Brits love the district popularly known as the Zona Inglesa ("English zone") with live music and

plentiful beer concentrated within the streets Mallorca, Londres and Gerona. The lavish show and revue programme with dinner in the Benidorm Palace (Av. Severo Ochoa 13 | tel. 9 65 85 16 60 | benidorm-palace.com) attracts a more reserved audience.

AROUND BENIDORM

5 ALTEA
10km / 15 mins by car via the N-332
This is where Spain takes on Greece. This small town (pop. 23,000) lies to the north-east of Benidorm and is the crowning glory of the Costa Blanca's coastal villages. There is plenty of activity around the marina and fishing port and along the Passeig del Mediterrani during the day, while at night the action shifts to the Old Town. In the summer, a trail of well-dressed, freshly showered people snakes its way up the steep climb through the narrow streets of the old town to the church square with its multiple cute boutiques, restaurants, bars and the Mirador de la Plaza de la Iglesia, a lookout point with a view stretching across the Med to Benidorm. As the light of the moon illuminates the whitewashed façades and tiled roofs it's not hard to imagine yourself on the Aegean Sea.

In the alleys around the plaza, designers (Altea is a city of creatives!) sell their unique pieces in small shops and, in the summer, at street stalls in

Altea's bijou old town

the evenings. A real fashion statement against Mango, Zara, Desigual and Co.! Tuesdays *(8am–2pm)* are market days. Looking for an honest opinion? You can safely leave the plastic stalls on C/ Camí de l'Algar. The fresh fruit and vegetables, almonds, olives and medlars that fill the stands on C/ Filarmónica, on the other hand, are fresh and regional. And don't worry, there are plenty of *churros*, the deep-fried, sugared Spanish goodness here too.

Tickled your tastebuds? Try *Cervecería Xeito de Goi (daily 12.45–5pm and 8pm–midnight | C/ San Pedro 35 | tel. 9 65 84 46 61 | €€–€€€)* on Altea's promenade, where landlady Goi Cortázar serves paper-thin fried artichoke hearts you could write poetry about, green asparagus with olive oil and coarse salt that are a revelation and deep-fired cod fillets that melt like butter on the tongue. The delicacies

INSIDER TIP
In seventh tapas heaven

whipped up by the Basque native and served by her daughters might not be cheap but are a real taste of heaven. On balmy summer evenings, there's no way around *Bar la Plaza (daily 12–3pm | Pl. de la Iglesia 12 | tel. 9 65 84 26 30 | €–€€).* Hidden away in the moonlit shadow of the church, the location belongs to Altea like the Prado does to Madrid and there's no better place to sip a mojito. On Fridays and Saturdays there's even live music!

A few beautiful beaches round off the package – not quite as fine and sandy as in Alicante, La Vila Joiosa or Benidorm, but less crowded. The choice of beaches ranges from the large *Platja de Cap Blanch* in the

Once besieged by crusaders and now by tourists: Guadalest

southwest (between Altea and Albir) to *Platja l'Olla* and the nudist beach *Platja de la Solsida*. 🗺 F9

6 FONTS DE L'ALGAR (FUENTES DEL ALGAR)

20km / 30 mins by car via the CV-70 and CV 715

It has so much potential. Let's put it this way: outside the high season and during the week, the Fonts de l'Algar are stunning. Thundering waterfalls, crystal-clear water, little bridges – it is not without reason that the Algar Springs near Callosa d'en Sarrià are promoted as a small natural paradise. But, with promotion comes overcrowding, at least in summer. Let's just say the restaurants are always full. You can usually get a general plan at the ticket booth but even without one you will not get lost on the network of paths leading upstream. It is also possible to go swimming in some places. The medlar products (juice, fruits preserved in syrup, honey and spirits) sold at the roadside stalls can be recommended. *July/Aug. daily 9am–8pm, June, Sept 9am–7pm, otherwise slightly varying according to the time of year 9am–5.30/6pm, Dec–Feb. 9am–3.30pm | admission 4–5 euros depending on time of year | lasfuentes delalgar.com*

INSIDER TIP
Delicacies from the medlar tree

From the Fonts d'Algar, it's well

worth enjoying the panoramic drive along the serpentine road and the picturesque mountain village of Tárbena to the *Coll de Rates (15km from the Fonts d'Algar)*, where the *Coll de Rates (daily 11am–6pm | Tel. 9 66 44 56 04 | Facebook: mirabela82 | €)* restaurant practically demands a break at the top of the pass. The view from the terrace is breathtaking! *F9*

7 GUADALEST ★

22km / 30 mins by car via the CV-70

Want to win a bet? Challenge your friends or family! Nobody, really nobody, would guess on a harmless spring afternoon that the village of Guadalest is subject to one of the largest touristic onslaughts in Spain. Nobody knows just how many tourists shuffle up the steps to the fortress of San José every year, because no one in the community of 240 inhabitants counts. Reports suggest, however, there are more than two million per year. After you get past the strip of souvenir shops, you enter a tunnel leading to the historical centre that is overlooked by a castle, Castell d'Alcozaiba, with its whitewashed bell tower. The views of the surrounding countryside are fantastic: the rugged mountains above and the turquoise Guadalest reservoir below in the valley.

Guadalest breaks another record too, with more museums than 99 percent of all other villages in Spain. Museums to visit include the folkloric *Museo Municipal Casa Orduña (daily in summer from 10am–8pm, otherwise until 6pm)*; the toy and puppet museum, *Museo Belén y Casitas de Muñecas (daily in summer from 10am–8pm, otherwise until 6pm)*, and the rather more unusual *Museo de Instrumentos de Tortura (in the summer open daily 10.30am–9pm, otherwise until 6pm)*, which features a collection of torture instruments. A museum that proves size doesn't matter is the *Museo de Microminiaturas (open daily 10am–8pm)*, which displays miniature works – such as Goya's *Naked Maya* on the wing of a fly – by the artist Manuel Ussá. Incredible! *F8–9*

8 ALCOI (ALCOY)

59km / 75 mins by car via the CV-70

Surrounded by mountains and with two nature parks, *Serra Mariola* and *Carrascar de la Font Roja*, only a stone's throw away, this small town (pop. 59,000) to the northwest is a popular inland destination. You should take the beautiful mountain route via Guadalest, Confrides and Benilloba on your way there. Alcoi's historical district, some of the Art Nouveau buildings, the Viaducto de Canalejas erected at the beginning of the 20th century and the *Archaeological Museum (Mon–Fri 9am–2pm, Sat/Sun 11am–2pm | admission 1 euro | Placeta de Carbo | alcoi.org/museu)* in the Old Town Hall (16th century) are well worth a visit. Crescents and crosses become Alcoi's every year in April/ May for the *Moros* y *Cristianos festivities*: these celebrate the battles between the Moors and Christians in the Middle Ages with one of the most archaic celebrations far and wide. ⌐ *E8*

🔟 LA VILA JOIOSA (VILLAJOYOSA)

15km / 20 mins by car via the N-332
Colourful house facades in orange, green, blue and red are the silent symbols of this small harbour town (pop. 35,000). The former fishing village is a seaside alternative to Benidorm. The small Old Town district with the *Assumpció Church* is charming; the *Moros y Cristianos* festival is celebrated here quite spectacularly as a sea battle between "Moors" and "Christians".

Right next to the fish action hall, the bar *La Lonja (daily | Ctra. del Port 37 | tel. 9 65 89 23 80 | €–€€)* plates up fish straight from the sea. If you've mastered any Spanish, you'll have no trouble striking up conversation with one of the fishermen at the counter – sailor's banter guaranteed!

INSIDER TIP
Fresh fish dished up

Last but not least, something sweet. After all, La Vila Joiosa is a connoisseur's paradise, as the town was once a giant chocolate factory. There were said to be at least 30 here at one time, with a handful remaining to this day. One of the best is ☯ *Chocolates Pérez (Partida Mediases 1 | Mon–Fri 9.30am–1.30pm and 5–7pm, Sat 9.30am–1.30pm | tel. 9 65 89 05 73 | chocolatesperez.com).* ⌐ *F9*

ALACANT (ALICANTE)

(⌐ E9–10) **The Romans were the first to enthuse about the special quality of the light that envelopes the city, today known as Alicante (pop. 335,000). Catch it early in the morning and late in the afternoon.**

OK, these days it shines over faceless high-rise buildings and deep concrete canyons, but also over beautiful promenades and parks like Monte Tossal and El Palmeral, as well as the fine sandy beaches of the provincial capital. The highlight of the city's rich heritage is *Santa Bárbara* Castle, but that is not all it has to offer – this coastal metropolis is anything but a stopover. Of course, Alicante is also a hub of plane and car travel, as well as a port for cruise ships and yachts. But there is so much more to it than that: beautiful cafes and quaint tapas bars cluster around the marina and Explanada d'Espanya, where you

WHERE TO START?

First of all, get in the mood by exploring **Alicante's marina**, then stroll along the Explanada de Espanya to the Old Town with the C/ Mayor and Cathedral. Afterwards, you can wander up to Santa Bárbara Castle. Car parks can be found on the Pl. Montanyeta and the Av. Alfonso X el Sabio, among others.

The Explanada d'Espanya in Alicante is perfect for a leisurely stroll

can see or be seen – whichever you prefer! The Sant Joan beach area is known throughout Spain as an attractive holiday destination.

SIGHTSEEING

OLD TOWN

Do want to kick-off your visit with some sightseeing? Best to start on the Explanada de Espanya, the bustling Rambla de Méndez Núñez or the small pedestrian precinct C/ Mayor (packed with bars, restaurants). Also check out the Baroque Town Hall (18th century) and the 17th-century *San Nicolás Cathedral*, with its 45-m blue dome. People really let their hair down here during the city festival celebrating Sant Joan (St John) around 20–24 June.

EXPLANADA DE ESPANYA

Somebody once counted them: the ground of Alicante's showpiece promenade is covered with 6.6 million pieces of marble in black and white and red tones. This is where everybody meets to indulge in their favourite activity: promenading in the shade of the palm trees and watching the comings and goings in the marina.

CASTELL/CASTILLO DE SANTA BÁRBARA ★ ⚑

It's a long way down from the castle complex on steep Monte Benacantil. It dominates the scene from an altitude of 166m above the city. The origins of the *castillo* can be traced back to the early Middle Ages when it was wrested from the Moors by the Spanish troops on Saint Barbara's Day in 1248. The highest section with the oldest

Castell de Santa Bárbara: crossbow at the ready!

remains is called La Torreta; part of the castle – with the dungeons and "Caves of the English" beneath it – is now used for the city museum, the *Museo de la Ciudad de Alicante*. There is a lift *(ascensor)* up to the castle from behind the Playa del Postiguet *(July/ August daily 10am–midnight, April– June and Sept 10am–10pm, at other times 10am–8pm)*. The view is absolutely spectacular!

MUSEU ARQUEOLÒGIC PROVINCIAL

Phoenicians, Iberians, Romans, Moors: for the most exciting encounters with Alicante's past, visit the Archaeological Museum. Enjoy the special night-time atmosphere in the

INSIDER TIP
Night at the museum

middle of summer when the museum stays open until late. *Sept–June Tue– Fri 10am–7pm, Sat 10am–8.30pm, Sun 10am–2pm, July/ Aug. Tue–Sat 10am–2pm and 6pm–midnight, Sun 10am–2pm | Plaza del Doctor Gómez Ulla 6 | marqalicante.com| ⊙ 1 hour.*

EATING & DRINKING

NOU MANOLÍN

This is one of the top addresses for gourmets – and has been since 1971! Mediterranean cuisine is prepared using the best traditional with a special touch. Reservations recommended! *Tue–Sat 1.15–4pm and 8.15pm–midnight, Sun 1.15–4pm | C/ Villegas 3 | tel. 965 20 03 68 | nou-manolin.com | €€€*

PESCA AL PESO

Warning: When hungry, the temptation to order way too much is strong here! A mouth-watering selection of fish and seafood is kept on display on ice – pick what you fancy and you'll be charged by weight, just like at the market. *Wed–Mon 1–4pm and 7–11pm | C/ Mayor 22 | tel. 9 65 98 13 72 | pescaalpeso.es | €*

SHOPPING

Fancy a culinary stroll? The well-stocked market *Mercat Central (Mon–Sat 9am–2pm | Av. Alfonso X El Sabio 8)* attracts everyone eager to buy or just take a look round. Find almost everything here from fresh fish, meat, vegetables, fruit and also a few small bars for tapas and maybe a drink in between. Another good option is the *Mercat Babel (Mon–Fri 7.30am–2pm, Sat until 3pm | C/ Asilo)*. There are additional catch-all markets *(mercadillos)* on some mornings, including the *Mercadillo Teulada (Thu 9am–2pm)* around the C/ Gran Vía and C/ Teulada. There is also an arts and crafts market well worth visiting in the summer on Sundays on the Plaza de Santa Faz *(10am–3pm)*.

BEACHES

The best beaches are to the north-east, beginning with the 90-m-long *Playa del Postiguet*; slightly smaller is the *Playa de la Albufereta*. The calm water of the *Playa de la Almadraba* makes the beach special and the small bays *(calas)* around *Cabo de las Huertas* have a great deal of charm. Far and away the most popular and longest beach is the ☆ *Platja de San Juan/ Playa de San Juan*, a 3-km sandy dream.

SPORT & ACTIVITIES

Boat trips to the *Isla de Tabarca* depart from the harbour run by companies such as *Cruceros Kontiki (tel. 6 86 99 45 40 | cruceroskontiki.com)*. There are a number of golf courses near Alicante, for example the *El Plantío Club de Golf (Ctra. Alacant–Elx, km 3 Partida Bacarot | tel. 9 65 18 91 15 | elplantio.com)* which offers two beautiful courses, each with 18 holes, 700m^2 of green space for putting practice and an area for practising chip shots. It also has a golfing school.

NIGHTLIFE

Alicante's castle has witnessed a lot of partying, especially in summer. The most popular places to go out and have fun are the marina with its cafés and pubs, the nearby Old Town and the *El Golf* area of the Playa de San Juan. Raucous parties and fiestas are held in the *Sala Stereo (C/ Pintor Velázquez 5 | salastereo.com)*. A good

INSIDER TIP
Rock 'n' roll

address for rock and pop, and occasionally rhythm & blues, is the *Rockbar Frontera (Av. Costa Blanca 140 | Playa de San Juan | rockbarfrontera.com)*.

AROUND ALACANT

🔟 SANTA POLA
19km / 20 mins by car via the N-332

Repeat visitors swear by Santa Pola (pop. 33,000). A plus point in this harbour town are the beach zones divided into Poniente and Levante. The beach *Gran Playa* in the Poniente section is 1km long and the 3.6-km long beach *El Pinet* stretches as far as the outskirts of the saline nature reserve. The *Playa La Gola* is more isolated.

On the newly built promenade at the yacht harbour, you will find smart restaurants and bars with terraces and panoramic views of the boats. Boats depart for the Isla de Tabarca throughout the year and there is a 🐋 Maritime Museum *(Museu del Mar | Mon–Fri 10am–4pm, also open afternoons in summer | 3 euros, children under 16 1.50 euros, children under 3 free | ⏱ 1 hour)* in the castle. Eight rooms teach children and grown-ups alike everything there is to know about navigation, mapping, maritime traditions and wooden boat building. Another attraction is the aquarium *(Acu- ario Municipal | Pl. Fernández Ordoñez | in summer daily 11am–1pm and 6–10pm, in winter Tue–Sat 10am–1pm, 5–7pm, Sun 10am–1pm | admission 3 euros, children under 16 1.5 euros, under threes go free)* near the harbour with all kinds of fish and plants. The old joke is that most of the species have been kindly donated by the fishermen of Santa Pola. 🗺 *E10*

1️⃣1️⃣ ILLA/ISLA DE TABARCA
11km / 35 mins from the harbour by boat

Wait, the pirates are long gone, right? Yes, but you'd be forgiven for forgetting that here! Set sail to the south from Alicante's harbour and you'll find the only inhabited Valencian island (pop. 80). In the 18th century, Spain's King Carlos III had the former pirate base fortified and sent families from Genoa to settle there. The ecologically significant water around the island is a protected marine reserve and is popular with divers. The island is almost 2km long and a maximum of 400m wide. The masses who descend in summer from Alicante or the closer Santa Pola on tourist boats are more interested in the fine sandy beach 🏖 *Platja Grande*, where you will find a dozen or so good fish restaurants. You might have to wait a while for a table during high season, but they're all worth it. For one of the 🦞 best lobster paellas, try *Casa Glòria (daily 9am–10pm | C/ Bernardo Ruso, 19 | tel. 9 65 97 05 84 | €€)*, which also has a branch down on the beach. We say nobody should leave without trying the specialty *Pata de pulpo frita*: fried octopus tentacles. Boat trips to Tabarca leave from Alicante, Benidorm and Santa Pola. 🗺 *E10*

ELX (ELCHE)

(🗺 D10) **Palms, palms – nothing but palms! There are almost as many palm trees as residents in**

Elche (pop. 232,000), located around 15km from the coast. The 200,000 magnificent specimens are protected by law.

Back in the 18th century, the palm forest right at the heart of the city, which dates back to the Moors, was home to almost a million trees. Today the forest is much smaller, but it's still the largest palm plantation in Europe. In 2000, the plantations were even declared a World Heritage Site by UNESCO.

SIGHTSEEING

BASÍLICA MENOR DE SANTA MARIA

The basilica from the 17th/18th century with its blue-tiled dome and dazzling gold altar is the venue of the *Misteri d'Elx* in August (see p.96). Visitors who climb to the top of the 37-m-high *tower (church daily 7am–1pm, 5.30–9pm | 30 mins, tower Mon–Sun 10.30am–3pm, in June–Sept 11am–7pm)* with its 170 steps are rewarded with a magnificent view.

BANYS ÀRABS

Over in the old town, you can dip into the remains of an underground Moorish bathing complex from the 12th century where people used to meet not only to wash but to socialise. *Tue–Sat 10am–2pm and 3–6pm, Sun 10am–2pm | Passeig de les Eres de Santa Llúcia 14*

A splash of colour on the rocky island of Tabarca

PALMERAR (EL PALMERAL) ★

In a word: palms. This name refers to all the magnificent date palms in Elche, which are to be found in many gardens in the town. The most popular of the palm parks begins behind the remains of the city walls and Moorish castle *Palau d'Altamira*: the *Parc Municipal* is well-furnished with paths, benches, flower beds, drinking fountains, a children's playground and music pavilion. The highlight of the palm groves however is the *Huerto del Cura (Mon–Sat from 10am, closing times vary by season: until 5.30/6.30/7.30/8pm or 2am | Admission 5.50 euros | Porta de la Morera 49 | huertodelcura.com)*. You can wander among palm trees, ponds, fountains and exotic plants in one of the most beautiful oases in Spain – a complex straight out of a picture-book that is classified as a "National Artistic Garden".

MUSEU D'ART CONTEMPORANI

Museum for contemporary art that's well worth a visit, showing works by Spanish avant-garde artists including Juana Francés and *Grup d'Elx. Tue–Sat 10am–2pm and 3–6pm, Sun 10am–2pm | Pl. Major del Raval s/n |* ⊙ *45 mins.*

DAMA DE ELCHE

When conversation turns to Elche in Spain, the "Lady of Elche" inevitably comes to mind. The bust is over 2,500 years old and is one of the single most valuable objects in Spanish cultural history and an outstanding testimony of Iberian art. While the original is in the *Museo Arqueológico Nacional* in Madrid, in Elche you'll still find the lady with her typical curls at every turn – for example, on the Glorieta promenade, in the town hall and, it goes without saying, on postcards and T-shirts.

EATING & DRINKING

MESÓN EL GRANAINO

Traditional cooking with an Andalusian touch. The restaurant also serves simple dishes such as potatoes prepared with spicy paprika *(pimentón). Closed Sun, Mon evenings and Aug | José María Buch 40 | tel. 9 66 66 40 80 | €–€€*

EL PERNIL

Delicious Mediterranean cuisine; fish and seafood are at the top of the menu – unsurprisingly! *Daily | Juan Ramón Jiménez 4 | tel. 9 66 61 33 03 | restaurantepernil.com | €–€€*

SPORT & ACTIVITIES

RÍO SAFARI ELCHE 🐒

Don't worry, there's something for the kids in Elche too! In this safari park they can meet exotic animals from lemurs to giraffes in the shade of thousands of palm trees. Most of the park is explored on foot, but the price also includes optional short round trips in the safari boat. The attractions include the crocodile farm and "reptile cave". There are usually two shows a day with parrots, sea lions and an elephant. The complex also includes a swimming pool, which is open in

The Huerto del Cura is a magical landscape of palms, cacti and ponds

summer. *In summer daily 10am–8pm, at other times 10am–6pm | admission 22.50 euros, children (3–12 years) 17 euros | Ctra. Elche–Santa Pola | Polígono 1 | riosafari.com*

AROUND ELX

🔢 GUARDAMAR DEL SEGURA
26km / 35 mins by car via the CV-853 and N-332

Situated at the mouth of the Riu Segura, this small town (pop. 15,000) encircled by belts of pine and eucalyptus trees, beaches and dunes, is a nature-lover's paradise. The *Parque Alfonso XII* is a splendid complex that starts directly behind the *Babilònia* and *Vivers* beaches and stretches as far as the marina and fishing port *Marina de las Dunas*. The park invites visitors to admire the remains from Phoenician times (*Yacimiento Fenicio*, eighth century BC) and the Moorish period (*Rabita Califal*, 10th century). The Old Town, founded in the 13th century and severely damaged in the 1829 earthquake, is behind the castle walls on the *El Castell hill*. The restaurants, bars and terrace cafés on the attractive promenades (*Av. d'Europa, Paseo Maritimo*) that run parallel to the *Platja Centre*, the central beach, are pleasant places to stop and take a break. The *Sunday flea market Mercadillo de El Campico (Sun*

9am–2pm | on the CV-895, turn-off from N-332 near El Moncayo) is held at the fairground near Guardamar.

Over 500 stalls offer everything possible: from fruit and vegetables, handcrafted objects and leather goods to inexpensive clothing. There is also international cuisine on offer, as well as beer, sangría and live music. *D10*

🔞 NOVELDA

17km / 25 mins by car via the CV-84

Set against a background of barren, rugged hills that appear to be straight out of a western, the area around Novelda (pop. 26,000), which is famous for its marble works, gives visitors a good impression of what life is like in the Spanish countryside. The cultural ensemble offered by the ☛ *La Mola* castle and *Santa María Magdalena Sanctuary* 3km out of Novelda at the foot of the 541-m-high Mola Peak is much more interesting than the city centre itself. The small, restored castle *(daily 10am–2pm, 4–7pm, in summer 10am–2pm, 5–8pm | free admission)* dates back to the days of the Moors and has two massive towers (12/14th century). The neighbouring Magdalena *sanctuary (same opening times as the castle)* is a completely different affair; construction was begun in 1918 based on a project by José Sala. The result is an ornate building with marble, quarry stones and brick arched windows in the Catalan style of Art Nouveau *Modernisme*. The light flows into the rather unassuming interior through red-and-white glass. *D9*

DRAMA IN THE CHURCH

Every year on 14 and 15 Aug, a liturgical drama accompanied by music is on the programme in Elche's Santa María Basilica: the *mystery play (Misteri d'Elx)* that has been performed since the late Middle Ages consists of two parts and has become a lavishly staged public spectacle. The play deals with the death of Christ, the Assumption and the coronation of the Holy Virgin and Mother Mary. Sophisticated equipment even makes it possible for the performers to hover through the space of the church. Tickets are also sold for the dress rehearsals on 11–13 Aug. In even-numbered years, there are additional dress rehearsals on 29 and 30 Oct. and an extra performance on 1 Nov. *misteridelx.com*.

🔞 TORREVIEJA

45km / 40 mins by car via the AP-7

In this area fishing and salt mining have been core sources of income for centuries, the Costa Blanca displays everything that makes it so attractive: beautiful beaches, a lively harbour and a well-developed tourist infrastructure. The coast and city (pop. 83,000) are separated into quite distinct districts, some of which are less inspiring than others. However, the *Sea and Salt Museum (Calle P. Pérez 10 | Wed–Sat 10am–2pm, Sun 10am–*

The Sanctuary of Santa María Magdalena stands on a hill near Novelda

pm), the submarine S-61 Delfín *(Tue–Sat 9.30am–1.30pm, children must be at least 1.15m tall |* ⏱ *30 mins)* that can be visited at the port and the cruises along the coast in excursion boats are all well worth a visit. An attraction for cyclists is the 7-km-long Vía Verde beginning at the historical railway station complex.

There are numerous restaurants here for sustenance, for example on the *Plaza Capdepont*. Night owls will find entertainment in the club area *Casagrande*, others can chill out at the *Marina Salinas*. Twice a year, in spring and autumn, Torrevieja celebrates its *Ruta de la Tapa (rutadelatapatorrevieja. com)*; over 30 restaurants offer creative, appetising snacks accompanied by a glass of wine or beer for 2 euros.

INSIDER TIP
Glorious mud Another wellness tip: the *Laguna de Torrevieja* provides the opportunity for relaxing mud baths free of charge. Give your skin a treat by rubbing the medicinally bene-fitting mud from the banks of the pink lagoon into your skin and allow it to dry. Then take a dip in the water which is warm all year round for a similar experience to the Dead Sea.

For the kids: Time to slip and slide for old and young alike at the 👪 *Aquópolis Torrevieja (early June–early Sept daily from 12pm, closing times range from 6pm in low season to 8pm in high | admission 26.95, children between 0.90–1.40m tall 22.95 euros (under 90cm free), cheaper tickets available online | Finca de la Hoya Grande | torrevieja.aquopolis.es).* The water park features the hair-raising "Kamikaze" where you rush down into cool water. "Speed" and "Boomerang" are also sure to set your pulse racing! 📖 *D11*

COSTA CÁLIDA/ MAR MENOR

HOT COASTLINE, COOL BEACHES

The "hot coast" really is a hot vacation tip: great bays flanked by rugged rocks, spectacular ribbons of sand and crystal-clear water. But the biggest draw of the Murcia region for holiday makers is that it hardly ever rains here in the summer, and the months of June, July and August bring guaranteed sunshine.

There are dozens of magnificent beaches and bays to choose from in the areas around Águilas and Mazarrón, but tourists will find twice as much pleasure in the La Manga del Mar Menor holiday region

With no waves and currents, the Mar Menor is perfect for water sports

with beaches, swimming spots and water-sports locations on both sides of their hotel: to the west, the inland sea, Mar Menor; to the east, the Mediterranean. Along with tourism, agriculture plays a major role here. The land produces lettuce, tomatoes, apricots, nectarines, grapes and peppers. Cartagena is the most important harbour city; numerous traces of its long history remain, including the Roman amphitheatre, the Forum Romanum, the Colosseum, not to mention reminders of settlement by the Iberians, Phoenicians and Moors.

15

Pliego

Alcantarilla

A7

Librilla

Alhama de Murcia

Aledo

Totana

23

2

REGIÓN DE MURCIA

A7

El Saladillo

Lorca

3

AP7

Mazarrón ★ 3

333-1

Bolnuevo Castellar

11

Ermita del Ramonete

332

Golfo de Mazarrón

AP7

Calabardina

Águilas
p. 108 Playa de las Delicias

MAR

MEDITERRÁNEO

102km 1 hr 10 mins

10 km
6.21 mi

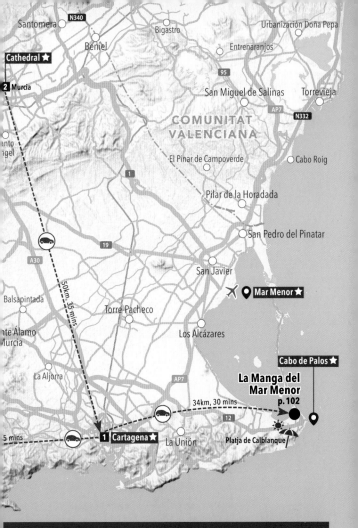

Santomera ○ ⬤N340 Bigastro ○ Urbanización Doña Pepa ○

Cathedral ★
2 Murcia

Béniel Entrenaranjos ○

⬤95

San Miguel de Salinas ○ Torrevieja

COMUNITAT
VALENCIANA ⬤AP7
⬤N332

anto
igel

El Pinar de Campoverde ○ ○ Cabo Roig

⬤1

Pilar de la Horadada ○

⬤19

○ San Pedro del Pinatar

A30

50km, 35 mins

Balsapintada ○

Torre-Pacheco ○ San Javier ○ ✈ ◉ **Mar Menor ★**

nte Álamo
Murcia

Los Alcázares ○

La Aljorra ○

⬤AP7 **Cabo de Palos ★**

La Manga del
Mar Menor
p. 102

34km, 30 mins

⬤12

5 mins **1 Cartagena ★** La Unión ○ **Platja de Calblanque** ◉

MARCO POLO HIGHLIGHTS

★ **MAR MENOR**
Vast lagoon: heaven for any water-sports
enthusiasts ➤ p. 102

★ **CABO DE PALOS**
Top-class diving and snorkelling on offer
➤ p. 103

★ **CARTAGENA**
Charming port with a Roman past
➤ p. 105

★ **MURCIA CATHEDRAL**
Stronghold of the faith in the heart of the
city ➤ p. 107

★ **BEACHES IN ÁGUILAS**
Promenade-lined beaches within the city,
beautiful bays beyond ➤ p. 110

★ **MAZARRÓN**
What a wonderful choice of sandy coves!
➤ p. 111

LA MANGA DEL MAR MENOR

(□ D12) **La Manga (pop. 17,000), complete with villas, apartment blocks and marinas large and small, is more like Dubai or even Florida than Spain. Guests are not so much by the sea, but in the sea, or at least between two seas, namely the Mediterranean and the ★ Mar Menor lagoon.**

The "sleeve", as La Manga translates, is a narrow 18.5-km spit of land that separates the Mar Menor from the Mediterranean. With an area of 170km², the Mar Menor is over eleven times the size of Lake Windermere and is considered the largest coastal lagoon in Europe. La Manga del Mar Menor, to give the town its full name, sprawls over the entire length of the spit and is crammed with villas and blocks of flats. It enjoys a reputation as a paradise for water-sports enthusiasts: kitesurfers can be seen streaking across the water, while divers submerge themselves beneath the waves of the Mediterranean. A permanent breeze blows along the spit that separates the two seas, and the sun shines from all sides: from the east in the morning and the west in the afternoon. It's true that this holiday spot is

Don't miss the underwater action around Cabo de Palos

anything but an insider's tip. In summer, the number of people in the area mushrooms to fill around 20,000 guest beds, but it's popularity is not without reason – the beaches here really are stunning.

The main road, *Gran Vía*, runs the length of the "sleeve", and addresses are usually indicated by the kilometre (e.g. "km 5") or appropriate exit (*salida*, e.g. "salida 37") along this route; the numbering begins in the south at the La Manga's only access road and runs north. The further north you go, the less there is going on. But be warned, you cannot drive all the way from Cabo de Palos in the south to San Pedro de Pinatar along La Manga – only via the mainland!

SIGHTSEEING

CABO DE PALOS ★

The cape with its lighthouse seems rather unremarkable at first, particularly as its beaches (and rocks) are usually crawling with people in summer. But Cabo de Palos, with its idyllic bays and crystal-clear water, is worth a second look. The marine reserve of Cabo de Palos and the Islas Hormigas, founded in 1995, are fabulously rich in marine flora and fauna, making it one of the most beautiful diving areas along the Mediterranean coast. The *Estación Náutica Mar Menor (tel. 9 68 57 49 94 | enmarmenor.com)* can provide information on all sorts of water sports and diving in the area and can recommend good diving schools.

EATING & DRINKING

DI MARE

Pleasant pizzeria nestled in the atmosphere of the marina – enjoyable spot with a terrace. *Daily | Puerto Deportivo Tomás Maestre | tel. 9 68 14 02 00 | dimare.es | €*

EL PEZ ROJO

This traditional restaurant ("The Red Fish") has a wonderful view of the sea. As expected, it serves primarily fish and seafood galore. *Daily | Paseo Marítimo 3 | Cabo de Palos | tel. 9 68 56 31 09 | €€-€€€*

LA TANA

The terrace at the port is a great spot for lunch. Excellent fish set the tone in this restaurant. *Daily 9.30am–midnight, in winter until 10.30pm | Cabo de Palos | Paseo de la Barra 3 | tel. 9 68 56 30 03 | la-tana.com | €€-€€€*

BEACHES

The Mar Menor is famous for its beautiful beaches. The shelving sand, with long hazard-free access, and the shallow water (maximum depth 7m) make the inland sea particularly suitable for families with small children and for water-sports enthusiasts. On the other side of La Manga, the Mediterranean Sea offers crystal-clear water and long sandy beaches, making it a dream for snorkelers and divers. A good name to remember is the *Platja de Calblanque*, regarded as one of

INSIDER TIP Beach pearl

Spain's most beautiful beaches, located about 11km south of La Manga on the Mediterranean. The sandy beach really is the stuff of dreams. But note that direct access to the beach by car is not possible in high season. Instead, there is parking on the RM-12 (exit Calblanque), from where buses will take you to the beach *(parking 4 euros, return bus ticket 3 euros, travel time approx. 8 mins)*.

SPORT & ACTIVITIES

Diving courses and special excursions, sometimes including night dives and wreck-diving, are organised e.g. by *Planeta Azul (Dimas Ortega 24 | Cabo de Palos | tel. 9 68 56 45 32 | planeta-azul.com)*. Sailing and wind-surfing equipment hire is the business of the *Escuela de Vela Sandrina (Gran Vía de la Manga, km 5.3, Edificio Orfeo | tel. 9 68 14 13 27 | Facebook: escuela sandrina.com)*. Courses are offered too. A good alternative is *La Manga Surf (Gran Vía | Acceso Isla de Ciervo, salida 23 | tel. 9 68 14 53 31 | mangasurf. com)*. Kite surfers will find excellent options at the *Kite Center La Manga (Gran Vía, km 2 | Edif. Costa Manga III | tel. 9 68 56 31 77 | kitecenter.es)*.

LA MANGA CLUB

No list of the region's sports options would be complete without La Manga Club. This luxurious hotel to the south of Mar Menor not only offers top-notch accommodation, nine restaurants and the Piano Bar. It also has three (!) 18-hole golf courses, countless tennis courts, football pitches, a cricket pitch and rugby grounds. But that's not all: Spa La Manga Club takes relaxation and pampering to another level. The club within the club is a luxurious wellness oasis with sauna, steam bath, indoor pool and whirlpool. *Los Belones | tel. 9 68 33 12 34 | lamangaclub.com*

NIGHTLIFE

The most popular trendy places to spend the evening hours are particularly around the *Tomás Maestre Marina (Gran Vía, km 14)* and near *Zoco de Levante (Gran Vía, salida 37)*. *Cabo de Palos* is also an established hotspot for going out in the evening.

AROUND LA MANGA DEL MAR MENOR

1 CARTAGENA ⭐

34km / 30 mins by car via the Autovía de la Manga (RM-12)

The harbour city of Cartagena (pop. 215,000) looks back on over 2000 years of history. Alongside the cities of Tarragona and Sagunt (p. 69), Cartago Nova as the ancients called it, was one of the most important ports and bases of the Roman Empire. Although numerous new buildings have been constructed over the old structures, the historical sites and stories remain, for example at the *Punic city wall* (*Muralla Púnica*), which has a great information centre (*July–mid-Sept Mon–Fri 10am–8pm, March–June and Sept–Nov Tue–Sun 10am–7pm, Nov–March Tue–Sun 10am–5.30pm | C/ San Diego 25 | ☉ 1 hr*) and the *Cerro Molinete* archaeological park.

One of the most prominent sights is the Roman amphitheatre, *Teatro Romano* (*May–Sept Tue–Sat 10am–8pm, Sun 10am–2pm, Oct–April Tue–Sat 10am–6pm, Sun 10am–2pm | admission 6 euros, children 3 euros | Pl. del Ayuntamiento 9 | teatroromanocartagena.org*), which could once host 6,000 visitors. The amphitheatre and its accompanying 🍦 museum are well worth a visit. But the story behind the amphitheatre's discovery is even more interesting. Back in 1988, a group of workers found a Roman inscription on a stone block during construction for a new arts and crafts centre in the middle of the old town, but they initially thought

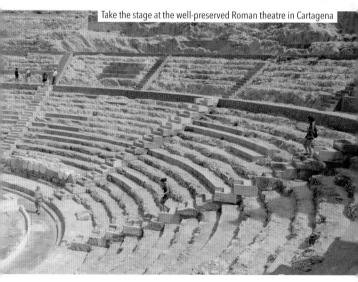

Take the stage at the well-preserved Roman theatre in Cartagena

nothing of it. In 1990 some sensational news followed: researchers believed an entire and presumably excellently preserved Roman theatre was buried right at the heart of the old town. And they were right. For years, the archaeologists dug and shovelled away to reveal the "Miracle of Cartagena", before the very first visitors were finally allowed into the perfectly preserved round structure in 2008.

You can also find traces of the Romans in the *Casa de la Fortuna (Apr–Dec Tue–Sun 10.30am–3.30pm, Jan–March Sat, Sun 10.30am–3.30pm | admission 2.50 euros | entrance at the Plaza del Risueño | ⏱ 30 mins)*, a residence dating from the first century BC containing mosaics; in the *Augusteum (Information about opening times in the Casa de la Fortuna | C/ Caballero)*, where the clergy met during the first and second centuries AD; and in the well-stocked *Archaeological Museum (Tue-Fri 10am–2pm, 5–8pm Sat/Sun 11am–2pm | C/ Ramón y Cajal 45 | museoarqueologicocartagena.es | ⏱ 45 mins)*.

The castle hill, topped by the *Castillo de la Concepción (July–mid-Sept daily 10am–8pm, Nov–March Tue–Sun 10am–5.30pm, at other times Tue–Sun 10am–7pm | admission 3.75 euros, children 2.75 euros)* offers the best views of the theatre, docks and surrounding mountains. The hills, which are easily reached by a panoramic lift, are the coolest part of the city in summer and thus very popular with locals. At the station at the bottom of the panoramic lift, you will see

the entrance to a former bunker from the Spanish Civil War – now a museum *(Refugio-Museo de la Guerra | July–mid-Sept daily 10am–8pm, Nov–March Tue–Sun 10am– 5.30pm, at other times Tue–Sun 10am–7pm | admission 3.50 | C/ Gisbert 21)*.

The 🐟 *Regional Museum of Modern Art (Museo Regional de Arte Moderno | Tue–Fri 10am–2pm and 5–7pm, Sat 11am–2pm and 5–8pm, Sun 11am–2pm | Palacio de Aguirre | Pl. de la Merced 15 | museosregion demurcia.es)* is a great spot for all art fans, and it's free of charge. The 🐟 *Museo Nacional de Arqueología Subacuática (mid-April-mid-Oct. Tue-Sat 10am–9pm, otherwise until 8pm, Sun 10am–3pm | Paseo Alfonso XII 22 | murciaturistica.es | ⏱ 1 hour)* is also free from 2pm on Saturday and all day on Sunday. It displays treasures recovered from under the sea, including amphorae and ivory from Phoenician and Roman times.

Most restaurants, cafés and popular evening meeting points are located on the seafront, where regular *tours of the harbour* on the tourist boat leave during the day. You can taste one of the best paellas in the region at the restaurant *Columbus (daily, closed Tue in the winter | C/ Mayor 18 | tel. 9 68 50 10 68 | €€)*. 🕮 D12

2 MURCIA

71km / 50 mins by car via the AP-7 and the A-30

The regional capital (pop. 440,000) on the Río Segura is in the middle of a large fruit-and-vegetable-growing region. The town can look back on

Murcia's cathedral combines architectural features from many periods of history

1,200 years of eventful history. Its first rulers were the Moors, who enclosed the settlement within a massive mantle of walls and named it *Mursiya*. They remained in control until well into the 13th century. The Christians then moved in and, in 1394, began construction of the magnificent ★ *Cathedral*, which is still Murcia's most important architectural monument. Its 90-m-high tower is the visible symbol of the city. The architecture of the house of worship displays both Gothic and Baroque styles; the interior decoration of the *Capilla de los Vélez* is particularly extravagant. Anyone interested in art and cultural history should also pay a visit to the *Cathedral Museum (Museo de la Catedral | Tue–Sat 10am–5pm, Sun 10am–1pm)* and the interesting *Museo de Santa Clara (Tue–Sat 10am–1pm, 4–6.30pm, Sun 10am–1pm, July/Aug. only Tue–Sun 10am–1pm | Av. Alfonso X el Sa-bio I)*, which is part of the historical complex of Santa Clara monastery.

A visit to the *Museo Salzillo (Thu–Sat 10am–2pm and 5pm–1am, closed Aug | Plaza de San Agustín 3/C/ Doctor Quesada | museosalzillo.es)* is especially worthwhile. It includes an exhibition from the oeuvre of the local Baroque sculptor Francisco Salzillo (1707–1783) The *Museum of Fine Arts (Museo de Bellas Artes) (C/ Obispo Frutos 12 | Tue–Fri 10am–2pm, Sat 11am–2pm and 5–8pm, Sun 11am–2pm | entrance free | ⊙ 1 hr)* focuses on paintings from the Renaissance and Baroque periods. Right at the heart of Murcia, Javier Cerezo puts on regular original exhibitions at the *Babel* gallery *(babelarte. com)*.

ÁGUILAS

Murcia's appeal is not only due to its many cultural attractions. Treat yourself with a bit of me-time at the wonderful spa *Balneario de Archena (balneariodearchena.com)* near Murcia. Whether you choose algae baths or aqua balancing, massages or exfoliation, relaxation is guaranteed. Plus, at 2,000 years old, the famous spa is one of the oldest on the entire Iberian Peninsula.

The local population is fond of celebrating, and the number of young people studying here guarantees that the city is always full of life. The Plaza Santo Domingo, Plaza Cardinal Belluga and Plaza de las Flores, with their excellent tapas bars and restaurants, are among the most boisterous areas. There are also tasty titbits and a daily set menu in the café-bar *Roses & Rosell (7am–11.30pm daily | Plaza de Camachos 16 | tel. 9 68 93 39 70 | €).* ⌕ C11

(⌕ B13) **Águilas (pop. 35,000) is a charming town, right on the border with Andalusia, that has still managed to preserve much of its traditional charm. But this is no empty platitude. People still meet, just as they always have, in the bars and on the promenade for a chat, and they still sit down and relax in the shade of the tropical greenery on the Plaza de España to enjoy the view of the harbour and the castle.**

Águilas looks back on a Roman past, as can be seen in the ruins of some Roman baths on C/ Canalejas. It attracts its fair share of tourists, but it's still quieter here than in some other coastal towns. And the best part? There are more than three dozen wonderful beaches in the immediate vicinity.

Águilas is situated on a sheltered bay

However, once the carnival season gets underway, normality is turned on its head! No less than 100 *peñas* (friendship groups) uphold the old traditions; they start preparing their extravagant costumes in summer and inject the fancy parades with enough flair to rival the carnival in Rio *(carnaval deaguilas.org)*. There is also a carnival museum *(Museo del carnival | C/ Pizarro, Bajo 1, Edif. La Torre | by appointment only: tel. 9 68 49 32 87 | free admission)* which you can visit all year round.

SIGHTSEEING

AUDITORIO

Even if modern architecture just isn't your thing, this building on the promenade will surprise you! Who would expect such big-city architectural flair in a small town like Águilas? The congress and event centre "Infanta Doña Elena" takes the shape of a sail caught in the wind. Inside, there is space for 650 spectators for concerts, musicals or operas. *C/ Aire 153 | auditorio aguilas.org*

CASTILLO DE SAN JUAN DE LAS ÁGUILAS

The fortress that dominates the town was built in the 16th century on the ruins of an earlier Moorish building, initially to provide protection from pirates, and was renovated in the 18th century. At the time, there was a latent fear of being attacked by the Turks and Berbers. The impressive fortress complex is divided into three sections and guarantees splendid views over the city and bay. *Tue–Fri 10am–1pm, 6–9pm, Sat/Sun 10am–2pm, 6–9pm, in winter Tue–Fri 10am–1.30pm, 4–6pm, Sat/Sun 10am–2pm, 4–6pm | above Plaza de España | ⊙ 2 hrs.*

EMBARCADERO DEL HORNILLO

In the bay of Hornillo, around 2km from the centre, this historical loading pier extends spectacularly far out into the sea. Built in 1903 by a British rail company, this construction enabled ferrous minerals to be loaded directly onto the trains. The daring technical construction of its time is now a designated historical monument.

EATING & DRINKING

BAR DE FELIPE

This restaurant is an institution in Águilas and is very popular with the locals. It serves delicious tapas, including sardines and tuna. A speciality of

Taste of the sea

the house is dried octopus *(pulpo seco)*. *Daily 10am–midnight | Plaza Alfonso Escámez 1 | €*

CASA DEL MAR

Fish restaurant behind the port. Recommended starters include salads *(alcaparras*, capers, are a typical dish)*, or *raciones* of octopus *(pulpo)* or shrimps and garlic in oil *(gambas al ajillo)*. Depending on the day's catch, the main courses are sea bream *(dentón)* or sea bass *(lubina)*. The restaurant also serves rice dishes. *Daily 1.30–4pm | Explanada del Puerto s/n | tel. 9 68 41 29 23 | €€*

LA VELETA

La Veleta is very popular with the locals on account of its fried octopus *(pulpo frito)*. *Mon–Sat 8.30am–11.30pm | C/ Blas Rosique 6 | tel. 9 68 41 17 98 | €€*

BEACHES

The ★ beaches here are a dream: delightful fine sand is the name of the game at the ✦ *Playa de las Delicias* in the main bay, between the port and the rock formations around the remarkably shaped *Pico L'Aguilica*. The climb up to the lookout point on the rock is well worth the effort. There are two other popular beaches: the *Playa de Poniente* and *Playa de la Colonia*; both are south-west of the castle hill and flanked by beautiful promenades. Further to the south-west, the main road in the direction of the Andalusian province of Almería leads to picturesque spots known as Cuatro Calas, the "four bays" (including *Higuerica* and *Carolina*). There are other beautiful beaches and bays waiting to be explored on both sides of *Cabo Cope* north-east of the town; one of the loveliest is *Playa de Calabardina*. An additional attraction behind the Playa del Hornillo east of the inner city is the *Rincón del Hornillo*, which has a flight of steps decorated with mosaics.

SPORT & ACTIVITIES

Diving courses, including night diving and diving sessions around the Isla del Fraile, can be booked at *Escuela de Buceo Estela (Paseo de Parra 38 | tel. 9 68 44 81 44 | escueladebuceo. com)* or alternatively at the *Centro de Buceo La Almadraba (C/ Ernest Hemingway 13 | tel. 9 68 41 96 32 | buceoalmadraba. com)* in the district of Calabardina. You can hire bicycles from *Mountain Bike (C/ Barcelona 1 | tel. 9 68 41 39 84 | cycling-friendly.com)*.

NIGHTLIFE

There are concerts of all types held at the *Casa de la Cultura Francisco Rabal*, the municipal cultural centre located on the Plaza Asunción Balaguer, named after Águilas' best-known son, the actor Francisco Rabal (1926–2001). The modern *Auditorio* behind the Playa de las Delicias is another destination for culture lovers.

Stone sculptures carved by nature, near Mazarrón

AROUND ÁGUILAS

8 MAZARRÓN ★

38km / 35 mins by car via the RM-D14 and the AP-7

The next highlight on the Costa Cálida is Mazarrón (pop. 32,000). The town is split between the coastal zone *Puerto de Mazarrón* and a small district 5km inland. The town is located in the bay of the same name, between Cabo Tiñoso and Cabo Cope.

It has a small fishing port, two marinas and a kilometre-long sandy beach. In fact, the place is a whopping 35km long if you add up all the beaches. Well worth seeing are the 19th century tow hall and the 16th century San Andrés church, although the main nave is all that remains of the original building. That said, it has a beautiful, coffered Múdejar ceiling. But the real attraction is the coast, with its string of sandy bays. *Castellar* and *Bolnuevo* beaches are absolutely dreamy. The *Erosiones de Bolnuevo*, bizarrely eroded stone formations carved by the wind and weather over the centuries, are a short distance away from Bolnuevo beach. There are designated areas for naturists *(calas nudistas)* to the south-east. In the summer, various open-air concerts are held on the beaches, *(mostly Fri/Sat)* at locations such as the *Playa del Puerto*.

Puerto de Mazarrón hosts a street market on Sunday mornings in the area around C/ Parque de Doñana – a great stop for reasonably priced clothes, shoes and fruit. C12

DISCOVERY TOURS

Do you want to get under the skin of the region? Then our discovery tours provide the perfect guide – they include advice on which sights to visit, tips on where to stop for that perfect holiday snap, a choice of the best places to eat and drink, and suggestions for fun activities.

❶ THROUGH THE HUERTA DE VEGA BAJA

➤ Meet the artists who work from caves
➤ Tapas and wine tasting
➤ The splendour of yesteryear: from palaces to monasteries

📍 Torrevieja	🏁	Doña Monse/Torrevieja
🔄 145km		2 days, 2½ hrs total driving time

ℹ️ Costs: approx. 100 euros for accommodation, 10 euros for petrol, 15 euros (per person) for wine tasting
Wine tasting at the ❸ Bodegas Cerdá Mon–Fri only; Bishop's Palace and the monastery Santo Domingo in ❹ Orihuela are closed Mon

A colourful façade in Cartagena

A ROUND TRIP OF CONTRASTS

The tour begins in ① Torrevieja ➤ p. 96 at the Casino Cultural *(Paseo Vistalegre 14)*. The historical cultural society building is impressive with its Moorish inspired mosaics. Enjoy breakfast before *starting off on the CV-905 to Rojales*. The ② Cuevas del Rodeo have become a meeting point for the art scene: around two dozen artists and craftsmen have set up studios here and the sculptor Carlos Carmona's Bar 10 is open at the weekend.

ÌDER TIP
Cave art

You continue your route through fields of artichokes on the CV-860 and CV-9302 to San Fulgencio which you pass by on your way to the nature reserve El Hondo. Then you *continue on the CV-859 and CV-9218 in the direction of San Felipe Neri before you drive parallel to the motorway via the CV-904/N 340 to Crevillent. The N-325 leads up into the Vinalopó hills. Just before Aspe, the CV-845 forks off at a sharp angle towards Hondón de las Nieves (El Fondó de les Neus). At the end of the village,* you will see the winery ③ Bodegas Cerdá *(Mon–Fri 10am–2pm, 4–8pm, Sat 9am–2pm, Sun 10am–2pm, reservation recommended | tel. 9 65 48 01 07 | bodega-scerda.com)* where you can join a guided

DAY 1
① Torrevieja

15km

② Cuevas del Rodeo

45km

③ Bodegas Cerdá

21km

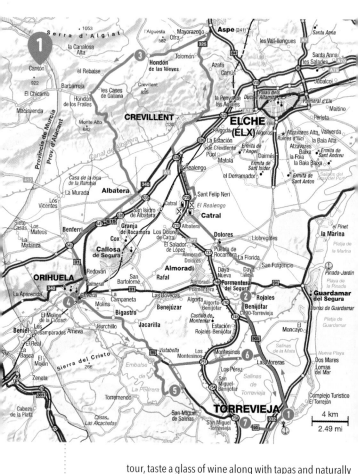

tour, taste a glass of wine along with tapas and naturally also buy some wine. *The route continues via Hondón de los Frailes and then turn left on the CV-873 to Albatera and via the N-340 to* **④ Orihuela**. Stay at the beautiful old town palace Sercotel Palacio de Tudemir (C/ Alfonso XIII 1 | sercotelhoteles.com | €€).

④ Orihuela

DAY 2

The next morning, you should pay a visit to the Museo Diocesano de Arte Sacro at the Palacio Episcopal (Mon–Sat 10am–6pm | admission 4 euros C/ Ramón y Cajal s/n | museodeartesacro.es) and the Bishop's Palace built in 1558. The monastery Santo Domingo (closed

Sat/Sun | admission 2 euros | C/ Adolfo Clavarana 51) dating from the 16th century is situated on the hill above the city and was used as a university from 1610 bis 1824. The small restaurant El Tranvía *(Av. España 8 | Tel. 9 66 28 03 20 | €€)* is centrally located.

21km

Now continue on the CV-95 via Bigastro towards Torrevieja. A worthwhile detour can be made to the reservoir La Pedrera. *The CV-950 winds its way in hairpin bends along the eastern bank of the lake until you reach the CV-951 after 10km. On your return to the CV-95,* you will see the adventure park ❺ Lo Rufete *(Ctra. Torrevieja–Orihuela, CV-951 km 1 | lorufete.com).* The restaurant ❻ La Herradura *(open daily | Av. Del Mar s/n | tel. 9 66 72 10 78 | €€–€€€)* in Los Montesinos is recommended for a stylish dinner in a former finca. End the day in Torrevieja with a drink on the terrace of the hotel ❼ Doña Monse *(C/ Raúl F. Giménez 75, Urb. Los Balcones | hotelmonse. com)* with a beautiful view across the salt lagoon.

❺ Lo Rufete
❻ La Herradura
14km

❼ Doña Monse

❷ DISCOVERING THE MURCIA REGION

➤ Urban flair in Cartagena
➤ Mining history, fortresses and spectacular cliffs
➤ Travel back in time to the Middle Ages

📍 Cartagena   🏁 Murcia

→ 260km   🚗 3 days, 4hrs total driving time

ℹ️ Costs: approx. 350 euros for accommodation, petrol, admissions for two
The Museo Minero in ❷ La Unión and the Restaurante Mares Bravas in the ❸ Cala Cortina are closed on Mon

STROLL, WATCH, ENJOY

❶ Cartagena ➤ p. 105 offers so much to see that you should plan a whole day for sightseeing. Walk along the

DAY 1
❶ Cartagena

Harbour Promenade at the Paseo Alfonso XII and the Calle Mayor, an elegant pedestrian zone with numerous street cafés. On the right, you will see the imposing Teatro Romano. You will be rewarded with a magnificent view over the harbour on your way up to the castle, the Castillo de la Concepción. An atmospheric bodega is the Restaurante Catedral *(closed Mon | Plaza Condesa de Peralta 7 | tel. 8 68 06 65 58 | lacatedralcartagena.com | €€)*. In the evening, everyone first congregates in the Old Town with tapas bars and restaurants and then in the Harbour Promenade with its numerous cafés and bars attracting you to chill out to live music.

DAY 2

22km

❷ La Unión

Before driving on to Águilas, it is well worth *taking a diversion via the winding coastal road N-343 to* ❷ La Unión, a traditional mining centre. Visit the Museo Minero *(Mon-Sat 10am-2pm | admission 3 Euro | C/ Mayor 55, Ed. del Liceo de Obreros)*. There is a monument to the miners by artist Estebán Bernal on Plaza Joaquín Costa in front of the market hall of the *mercado público*, which is also worth a visit. *The mountain road to La Unión and back to the coast at Puerto Escombreras is full of hairpin bends.* Go for a swim at the idyllic ❸ Cala Cortina and then eat fish in the Restaurante Mares Bravas *(daily 9am-8pm | tel. 9 68 50 20 65 | maresbravas.es | €€)*.

22km

❸ Cala Cortina

36km

WHERE THE CANNONS ARE

Back on the N-332, you drive through Cartagena and take the E 22 on the left via Canteras to the nature park La Muela-Cabo Tiñoso. Before the country road leads down into the bay of Mazarrón, turn left to the ❹ Batería de los Castillitos, a fortress situated on a hilltop. Look out for the two 18-m-long cannons. *From here, you drive on to Puerto de Mazarrón, through the town and reach the suburb of Bolnuevo* where wind and weather have formed bizarre rock formations eroded on the coast – the spectacular ❺ Erosiones de Bolnuevo. *Mazarrón is linked to the harbour town of* ❻ Águilas ➤ p. 108 *by a country road of almost 60km in a beautiful landscape via the RM-332.* In Águilas, you can find a hotel and then go for a walk along the promenade to the viewpoint Pico L'Aguilica in the late afternoon.

❹ Batería de los Castillitos

24km

❺ Erosiones de Bolnuevo

45 km

❻ Águilas

CASTLES, CATHEDRALS & SPAS

North of Águilas, you drive along a bleak mountainous landscape to ⑦ Lorca, which has preserved its monumental heritage in the form of the medieval castle. North-east of Lorca, the A-7 crosses fertile plains and desert-like hills. Stop in ⑧ Alhama de Murcia, a place dominated by its hill castle to visit the archaeological museum *Los Baños (Tue–Sat 10am–2pm, 5–8pm | C/ Sánchez Vidal 5 | musealhamademurcia.es)* which offers an overview of over 2000 years of the history of thermal baths. The tour is rounded off with a visit to ⑨ Murcia ► p. 106. At the heart of the formerly Moorish Mursiya is the Santa Mariá Cathedral originally dating from the 14th century *(daily 10am–5pm | admission 5 euros | Pl. del Cardenal Beluga 1 | catedralmurcia.com)*. A lively pedestrian zone flanked by numerous shops and terrace cafés links the cathedral and the Segura River.

DAY 3	
43km	
⑦ Lorca	
39km	
⑧ Alhama de Murcia	
38km	
⑨ Murcia	

❸ HIKING IN THE SERRA D'IRTA NATURE RESERVE

➤ A Moorish watchtower stands as a landmark
➤ Picnic under pine trees
➤ Round it off with sun and sea on the beach

📍	Peñíscola	🏁	Peñíscola
🔄	24km	🥾	8 hrs, 6 hrs total walking time
📶	medium	↗	400m

ℹ The tourist information at Paseo Marítimo in ❶ Peñíscola provides a general map (also in English). Or you can download the map from: *peniscola.es/en* under "plan the trip".

AN EARLY START ...

Start this tour early in the day to escape the midday heat. *Follow the brown signs in the centre of* ❶ Peñíscola ➤ p. 44 *to the southern exit towards the* Serra d'Irta Nature Reserve ➤ p. 48 *crowned by the high Pico Campanelles rising up to 572m. After driving 3.5km, park the car near the junction leading to the left.* A section of asphalt is followed by a wide gravel ascending path which rises up over rocky outcrops, continues at a high altitude and finally leads to the ❷ Torre Abadum (also known as *Abadun* or *Badún*), a watchtower built by the Moors as a protection against pirates which was fortified in the middle of the 16th century. The round tower is 5.75m at is base and 11m high. Continue walking in the direction of the Playa Pebret. *Behind the round tower, a tarred road leads down to a pine tree grove and ascends again to the right a few hundred metres before the Playa Pebret. A sign indicates the parking area Mas del Senyor 3.5km away.* Here you turn away from the coast: the gravel path ascends steeply and you can look back at the sea. *Close to a country*

❶ Peñíscola
6km

❷ Torre Abadum
5km

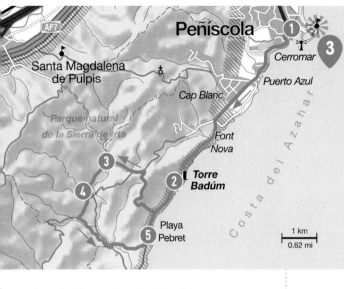

...house, the path twists again to the left and becomes wider. The parking area ❸ *Mas del Senyor* is ideal for a picnic in the shade of the pines. Here you can detect the scent of lavender, thyme, rosemary and sage and see miniature palms, mastic trees and broom growing.

BACK TO THE WATER

It is at least a further 1km to the ❹ Pou del Moro, the "Moorish fountain" slightly off the path which continues up and down through sparse forests of pine *and leads into a wide loop descending 4km to the coast. The path is indicated by yellow and white hiking signs and also head-high wooden stakes marked red at the top. At one point, the direction is not clear at a three-point triangle where you should take the route on the left.* The path gradually peters out in the direction of the sea and arrives at the track near the coast. *From the junction, it is only another few hundred metres to the left to the beach* ❺ El Pebret which invites you to take a dip in the sea before relaxing on the beach. Once you have regained your energy, you can continue back to the original starting point on the edge of ❶ Peñíscola with beautiful views of the Old Town crowning the hill of Peñíscola.

❸ **Mas del Senyor**

1km

❹ **Pou del Moro**

4km

❺ **El Pebret**

8km

❶ **Peñíscola**

GOOD TO KNOW

HOLIDAY BASICS

ARRIVAL

GETTING THERE

From the south of England, the main overland route **by car** is from Dover via Calais, Paris and Lyon to the Mediterranean and then past Perpignan and Barcelona towards the south. You will have to pay motorway tolls in France; in Spain there is a difference between the *autopistas* (motorways) that are subject to charges and the free *autovías* (main roads). You will find help on the internet from the free route planners such as *viamichelin.com*; they not only recommend various routes but also calculate the costs of the tolls you will have to pay in France and Spain.

Travelling **by train** from London to the Costa Blanca is possible, but it takes a long time and you will need to change in Paris and Barcelona. For

Type C

230 Volt, European-style two-pin plugs.

information on the connections between London and Barcelona, see *raileurope.co.uk* and *seat61.com*; information on railway travel in Spain is available under *renfe.com*.

Eurolines, part of the National Express service provides **coaches** from London to Alicante, but you have to change twice, once in Lille and once in Barcelona. You will also need a good book and a lot of patience. The advantage, however, is that the ticket is quite reasonable. For more information and price enquiries, see *nationalexpress.com*.

The international **airports** in the region are in València, Alicante and Murcia. All three are included in the

Sightseeing tour bus in València

flight plans of many airlines including British Airways, EasyJet and other carriers, with numerous connections depending on the season. There are also regular charter flights to Alicante and Murcia. Since 2014, budget flights with *Norwegian Airlines (norwegian. com)* have been introduced, departing from airports including London-Gatwick, Edinburgh, Dublin, JFK New York and other US cities to Alicante.

IMMIGRATION

Citizens of the UK & Ireland, USA, Canada, Australia and New Zealand need a valid passport but no visa to enter any country in the EU. Children below the age of 12 need a children's passport. Check online for the latest travel advice and entry requirements: *gov.uk/foreign-travel-advice* (UK Citizens) or *state.gov/travel* (US Citizens).

CLIMATE & WHEN TO GO

Clocking in at 300 sunny days a year and with rarely less than six hours of sunshine a day, Spain's south-east coast is a year-round destination. Even in winter, sunshine is a sure thing, although you should also pack warmer clothes, especially for the evenings. In summer, the region around Alicante and Murcia is particularly sunny and rain is extremely rare between June

RESPONSIBLE TRAVEL

Keen to keep an eye on your carbon footprint when travelling? For information on ways to offset your emissions, plan an eco-friendly route and show sensitivity to nature and culture, visit the following websites: *atmosfair.de/ en*, *myclimate.org*, *routerank.com* and *ecotourism.org*.

and August. In summer, the thermometer usually settles at around 30 degrees during the day and 17–19 degrees at night. The best months to travel are April–June and Sept/Oct.

GETTING AROUND

DRIVING

The road traffic accident rate in Spain is high; some drivers do not keep a safe distance or show consideration for other road users. As such, it is important to pay extra attention when driving. Those travelling by car must have their vehicle registration documentation *(permiso de circulación)*, proof of insurance and driver's licence to hand, as well as two warning triangles and a high-visibility vest in the car. The speed limit on main roads outside of built-up areas is 90 or 100 kmh (see signs), 120 kmh on motorways. In built-up areas, the speed limit depends on the number of lanes: 20kmh for a narrow single lane; 30kmh for two lanes and 50kmh for a dual- or multi-lane carriageway. Fines for speeding are substantial: from 100 euros for 20kmh over the limit and from 600 euros for over 50kmh. Driving using a mobile phone will set you back 200 euros, driving under the influence of alcohol, 500 euros. When parking, watch out for the colour: you can park on white spaces, while yellow markings and jagged lines signify no parking. Blue markings signal limits for specific cars (with parking disc or ticket). Orange areas are for residents and short-term parking only.

CAR HIRE

The standard car rental companies have offices at the international airports; you can save money if you compare prices on the internet and book before you leave. The companies have different minimum ages for those hiring a car, but it is normally 21. You will need to present a credit card. If you book early enough, you will get a small car for approx. 10 euros a day, including mileage and taxes in the pre-season, plus petrol. Spanish firms frequently attempt to attract customers with seemingly cheap prices, but they often operate with the trap of so-called "petrol politics" which conceal hidden extra costs. The "policy" is that the customer has to pay an additional sum for a full tank when he picks up the car – this can be around 40 euros upwards. The car can then be returned with an empty tank, but the amount charged before will be much higher than that needed to fill it up! To avoid unpleasant surprises, including an additional completely arbitrary "service charge" or insurance you have already taken out at home – you are advised to watch out for the phrase "rental firm charges additional costs" and instead choose a filter box for offers without additional charges.

PUBLIC TRANSPORT

Buses *(e.g. alsa.es)* are the most popular means of transport in the region, and there is an excellent network of

FESTIVALS & EVENTS
ALL YEAR ROUND

JANUARY
Epiphany (all over): processions through towns and villages; on the coast, the Three Wise Men often arrive by boat (5 January)

FEBRUARY/MARCH
Carnival (Águilas and elsewhere): *carnavaldeaguilas.org*

MARCH
★⚑ **Las Fallas** (València and elsewhere): Huge wood and papier-mâché creations are burned (around 19 March)

MARCH/APRIL
Semana Santa (all over): processions
Moros y Cristianos (Alcoi): end April

MAY
Feria de Mayo: (Torrevieja and elsewhere): Horse shows and flamenco

JUNE
Hogueras de San Juan (Benidorm, Dénia and elsewhere): Midsummer fire festival (24 June)

JULY
Patron saint's festival (Dénia)
Feria de Julio (València)
Moros y Cristianos (Guardamar del Segura)

AUGUST
Moros y Cristianos (Elche): around 8 August
★ **Misteri d'Elx** (Elche): mystery play *misteridelx.com*
Tomatina (Bunyol): messy tomato festival (last Wednesday of month)

SEPTEMBER
Feria (Murcia): with Moros y Cristianos
Fiestas de Cartagineneses y Romans (Cartagena): Festival of the Carthaginians and Romans

NOVEMBER
Fira/Feria (Cocentaina, province of Alicante): All Saints' Day celebration with concerts and medieval market

services. Buses are cheaper and run more often than trains. Each town has a bus stop or central bus terminus *(estación de autobuses)*. Alicante and València are on the AVE superfast train network for trains to/from Madrid *(renfe.com)*. The signposts *estación de Renfe* will guide you to the train station *(estación ffcc)*.

TAXIS
Pretty much every town has a taxi rank. The base fee is 1.30 to 1.40 euros, and the price per kilometre is 0.60 to 1.40 euros.

EMERGENCIES

EMBASSIES & CONSULATES
BRITISH EMBASSY
Paseo de la Castellana 259D, 28046 Madrid | tel. +34 9 17 14 63 00 | ukinspain.fco.gov.uk/en
There is also a British Consulate in Alicante *(tel. +34 9 65 12 60 22)*.

U.S. EMBASSY
Calle de Serrano 75, 28006 Madrid | tel. +34 9 15 87 22 00 | madrid. usembassy.gov
There is a U.S. Consulate in València *(tel. +34 9 63516973)*.

EMERGENCY SERVICES
National emergency number: tel. 112 National Police: tel. 091 Municipal Police: tel. 092 Guardia Civil: tel. 062

HEALTH
The European Insurance Card is valid in Spain. With it, you will receive treatment through the public health service but not through private providers; dental services are not included and you can't select your own doctor. To be on the safe side, you should take out travel insurance. It is important that the doctor treating you gives you an exact bill to enable you to get a refund when you return home; the same applies to any medicine you need.

SAFETY
Spain is a safe country, but there is still a risk of pickpockets and burglaries, so you should take the usual precautions. Car drivers should make sure that absolutely nothing is left visible in the car when it is parked – not even a map or sunglasses!

ESSENTIALS

ACCOMMODATION
Accommodation ranges from the simple *bed & breakfast (pension)* or *guesthouse (hostal)* to luxury hotels. *NH (nh-hotels.com)* and *Meliá (melia. com)* are good-value hotel chains. Stylish and very Spanish are the *Paradores (parador.es)*, state-run three-to five-star hotels within historic buildings. Country houses *(casa rurales)* are becoming increasingly trendy. *Casas Rurales (casasrurales. net)* and *Rusticae (rusticae.es)* specialise in providing such charming and

exclusive accommodation. Those on a tighter budget can stay in the youth hostels (reaj.com).

CAMPING

Campers will find good facilities on the coast. As well as the usual tent and caravan pitches, some sites also rent out bungalows. Not all campsites are open year round; some are only in operation from Easter to October. Information in English is available from: infocamping.com and spain camping.com

BANKS & DEBIT/CREDIT CARDS

Banks are generally open 9am to 2pm Monday to Friday. Credit cards such as Mastercard and Visa are widely accepted, and cash machines (caieros automáticos) are standard almost everywhere. When paying with a credit card, you may have to prove your identity.

BEACHES
NATURISM

Topless sunbathing might be standard on many beaches, but being completely nude is not. Naturists should go to the sections of the beaches or whole beaches specially reserved for this purpose (playas naturistas), e.g. Playas de la Olla and Solsida near Altea.

CUSTOMS

Travellers from the UK, USA, Canada, Australia or other non-EU countries are allowed to enter Spain with the following tax-free amounts for personal consumption: 200 cigarettes or 100 cigarillos or 50 cigars or 250g smoking tobacco. 2 litres wine and spirits with less than 22% volume alcohol, 1 litre spirits with more than 22% volume alcohol content.

Travellers to the United States who are returning residents of the country do not have to pay duty on articles purchased overseas up to the value of $800, but there are limits on the quantities of alcoholic beverages and tobacco products. For the regulations for international travel for U.S. residents please see http:// cbp.gov

INTERNET & WI-FI

Wifi is usually available free of charge at airports, in restaurants and, increasingly, in hotels, although some still charge guests for Wifi.

LANGUAGE

Two languages are spoken in the Communitat Valenciana: Spanish (i.e. Castilian or castellano) and Valencian, the second official language (see also p.128 Useful words & phrases).

OPENING HOURS

There are no strictly controlled opening hours in Spain. You can assume that shops are open 9.30/10am to 1.30/2pm and 4.30 to 8pm Monday to Saturday and also all day on Sunday in the tourist areas during the high season. The Spanish enjoy shopping in large supermarkets (hipermercados) on the outskirts of towns; they are open 10am to 10pm Monday to Saturday with no break for lunch. The opening hours of the post offices vary; some have a siesta in the afternoon but all close at around midday on Saturday.

Government offices are usually open 9am to 2pm Monday to Friday. If museums and monuments are open on public holidays, the opening hours normally adhere to Sunday opening times (also provided in this book).

PHONE & MOBILE PHONE

When calling abroad: dial *00* then the country code (UK *44*, US *1*, Ireland *353*), the area code without *0* and the number. The country code for Spain is *0034* followed by the telephone number. In Spain, expensive service numbers often start with *901* or *902*. Fixed numbers start with a *9*; Spanish mobile phone numbers start with a *6*. The largest mobile operators are Movistar, Vodafone, Orange and Yoigo. Roaming charges for UK visitors depend on your provider and your contract.

POST

Letters up to 20g and postcards to European countries usually only take a few days to reach their destination. Postcards within Europe currently cost 0.75 euros, a standard letter 1.65 euros. Stamps *(sellos)* are available from post offices and tobacconists *(tabacos)*.

PRICES

The price increases in recent years mean that Spain is no longer a country where everything is much cheaper than at home. However, some things have remained less expensive, including wine, public transport, fruit and vegetables. Most goods and services have a VAT *(IVA)* rate of 21 percent;

hotel, restaurant and taxis charge the reduced rate of 10 percent. Note that information on whether *IVA* is included in the bill is frequently given in very small print.

HOW MUCH DOES IT COST?

Coffee	*about 1.40 euros for a small cup of coffee with milk (cortado)*
Museum	*3–10 euros depending on the museum*
Leather shoes	*from 60 euros for brand footwear*
Daily set menu	*from about 8 euros in a simple restaurant*
Bus trip	*8–9 euros for 100km*
Ceramics	*from 4 euros for a small souvenir plate*

PUBLIC HOLIDAYS

1 Jan	Año Nuevo (New Year's Day)
6 Jan	Reyes Magos (Epiphany)
March/April	Viernes Santo (Good Friday)
1 May	Fiesta del Trabajo (Labour Day)
15 Aug	Asunción de Nuestra Señora (Assumption Day)
12 Oct	Día de la Hispanidad (Hispanic Day)
1 Nov	Todos los Santos (All Saints' Day)
6 Dec	Día de la Constitución (Constitution Day)
8 Dec	Inmaculada Concepción (Immaculate Conception)
25 Dec	Navidad (Christmas Day)

TIPPING

Spaniards are not huge tippers. Satisfied guests leave five to 10 percent extra in restaurants. In bars, you can round up the bill, but this is not necessarily expected. The chambermaids in hotels are happy with one or two euros per day. Taxi drivers don't expect tips.

TOURIST INFORMATION

In Spain, the local tourist offices *(oficina de turismo)* provide information.

SPANISH TOURIST OFFICES

UK: 64 North Row | London W1K 7DE | tel. +4420 73 17 2011
Canada: 2 Bloor Street West | Suite 3402 | Toronto, ON, M4W 3E2 | tel. +1 4169613131
USA: 60 East 42nd Street, Suite 5300 (53rd Floor) | New York, NY 10165-0039 | tel. +1 21 2265 88 22. In the U.S., there are additional offices in Chicago, Miami and Los Angeles.

WEATHER IN ALACANT/ALICANTE

High season
Low season

	JAN	FEB	MARCH	APRIL	MAY	JUNE	JULY	AUG	SEPT	OCT	NOV	DEC
Daytime temperature	16°	17°	19°	21°	24°	27°	30°	31°	28°	25°	19°	17°
Night-time temperature	5°	6°	8°	10°	13°	16°	19°	19°	18°	14°	7°	7°
Hours of sunshine per day	6	7	7	9	10	11	12	11	9	7	6	6
Rainy days per month	4	4	4	4	3	2	1	1	4	4	6	5
Sea temperature in °C	14°	14°	14°	15°	17°	20°	24°	25°	24°	21°	18°	15°

Hours of sunshine per day   Rainy days per month   Sea temperature in °C

WORDS & PHRASES
IN SPANISH

SMALLTALK

yes/no/maybe	sí/no/quizás
please/thank you	por favor/gracias
Hello!/Goodbye/See you soon	¡Hola!/¡Adiós!/¡Hasta luego!
Good morning/evening/night	¡Buenos días!/¡Buenas tardes!/¡Buenas noches!
Excuse me/sorry!	¡Perdona!/¡Perdone!
May I?	¿Puedo …?
Sorry?/Could you repeat?	¿Cómo dice?
My name is …	Me llamo …
What is your name? (formal/informal)	¿Cómo se llama usted?/¿Cómo te llamas?
I am from … the UK/USA/Ireland	Soy del Reino Unido/de los Estados Unidos/de Irlanda
I (don't) like this	Esto (no) me gusta.
I would like … /Do you have …?	Querría …/¿Tiene usted …?

SYMBOLS

EATING & DRINKING

The menu, please!	¡El menú, por favor!
expensive/cheap/price	caro/barato/precio
Could you bring ... please?	¿Podría traerme ... por favor?
bottle/jug/glass	botella/jarra/vaso
knife/fork/spoon	cuchillo/tenedor/cuchara
salt/pepper/sugar	sal/pimienta/azúcar
vinegar/oil/milk/lemon	vinagre/aceite/leche/limón
cold/too salty/undercooked	frío/demasiado salado/sin hacer
with/without ice/fizz (in water)	con/sin hielo/gas
vegetarian/allergy	vegetariano/vegetariana/alergía
I would like to pay, please	Quiero pagar, por favor.
bill/receipt/tip	cuenta/recibo/propina

MISCELLANEOUS

Where is ...?/Where are ...?	¿Dónde está ...? /¿Dónde están ...?
What time is it?	¿Qué hora es?
today/tomorrow/yesterday	hoy/mañana/ayer
How much is ...?	¿Cuánto cuesta ...?
Where can I get internet/WiFi?	¿Dónde encuentro un acceso a internet/wifi?
Help!/Look out!/Be careful!	¡Socorro!/¡Atención!/¡Cuidado!
pharmacy/drug store	farmacia/droguería
broken/it's not working	roto/no funciona
broken down/garage	avería/taller
Can I take photos here?	¿Puedo fotografiar aquí?
open/closed/opening hours	abierto/cerrado/horario
entrance/exit	entrada/salida
toilets (women/men)	aseos (señoras/caballeros)
(not) drinking water	agua (no) potable
breakfast/B&B/all inclusive	desayuno/media pensión/pensión completa
car park/multi-storey car park	parking/garaje
I would like to hire ...	Quiero alquilar ...
a car/a bike/a boat	un coche/una bicicleta/un barco
0/1/2/3/4/5/6/7/8/9/10/100/1000	cero/un, uno, una/dos/tres/cuatro/cinco/seis/siete/ocho/nueve/diez/cien, ciento/mil

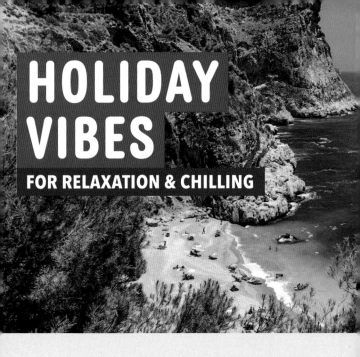

HOLIDAY VIBES
FOR RELAXATION & CHILLING

FOR BOOKWORMS & FILM BUFFS

📖 REEDS & MUD
Valencian author Blasco Ibáñez's (1867–1928) most famous novel details the life of rice farmers in the 19th century: a true Spanish classic.

📖 OR THE BULL KILLS YOU
The first in Jason Webster's highly acclaimed crime series featuring Chief Inspector Max Cámara of the València police. Combines a suspenseful detective thriller with a vivid portrayal of the city in the build-up to the *Fallas* celebrations (2012).

🎥 EL CID
Travel back in film history, to 1961 to be precise, and find this classic. Hollywood hero Charlton Heston plays legendary army leader El Cid, who reconquered Peñíscola from the Moors in the mid-16th century.

🎥 TOMORROWLAND
Some of the sequences in this science fiction film (2015) featuring George Clooney were filmed in València in the *Ciutat de les Arts i les Ciències*. 300 extras from València were included in the filming.

PLAYLIST

0:58

⏸ **AMARELA – ¿DESDE CUANDO?**
Spanish guitar and a voice to make your heart swell. The artist Amarela from Murcia is our insider tip from the coast

▶ **MARÌA DOLORES PRADERA – EL ROSARIO DE MI MADRE**
The great voice of Spain – perfect for a romantic evening in the light of the silver moon over the Mediterranean Sea

▶ **ROSANA – EL TALISMÁN**
The most beautiful song from this Spanish singer, taken from her best-selling album *Lunas rotas* (1996) – sure to get you in a good mood!

▶ **SOLE GIMÉNEZ – SIGO ESPERANDO LA LLUVIA**
Beautiful song from one of the best singers of Spanish pop – the perfect soundtrack to a late night!

The holiday soundtrack is available on **Spotify** under **MARCO POLO** Spain

Or scan the code with the Spotify app

ONLINE

COSTACALIDACHRONICLE.COM
Information in English about the Costa Cálida, including budget tips.

COSTA-NEWS.COM
The website of Costa Blanca's local English-language weekly newspaper includes a selection of news stories and all the classified ads.

HOLAVALENCIA.NET
English-language blog for València; regularly updated lists of the top five sights, restaurants, things to do, etc., with city map, videos and forum

INFOCOSTABLANCA.COM
Offers practical advice; the climate page has current data from weather stations.

HTTP://LAMARINAFORUM.COM
A general Costa Blanca forum for the English-speaking community; topics range from news to learning Spanish.

VALENCIA MAP & WALKS
Explore València with this iPhone app

VISITVALENCIA.COM
Official tourism website for València, also available as a free app

TRAVEL PURSUIT

THE MARCO POLO HOLIDAY QUIZ

Do you know your facts about the Costa Blanca? Here you can test your knowledge of the little secrets and idiosyncrasies of the region and its people. You will find the correct answers below, with further details on pages 16 to 25 of this guide.

❶ What is the stereotypical view of Valencians?
a) They are stubborn and punctual
b) They are grumpy and reserved
c) They are lively and chatty

❷ How many days of sunshine does the Costa Blanca have each year?
a) 300
b) 140
c) It's rarely sunny here

❸ What is the name for the Spanish version of Art Nouveau?
a) Modernisme
b) Clasicismo
c) Estilo juvenil

❹ Which animals are driven through the streets to celebrate local patron saints in the countryside?
a) Sheep and goats
b) Hares and hedgehogs
c) Bulls and cows

❺ How long did the Moorish period in Spain last?
a) 781 years
b) 481 years
c) 100 years

❻ Who was Joaquín Sorolla?
a) A famous Impressionist painter
b) A Dominican penitential preacher
c) A Spanish footballer

Answers: 1c, 2a, 3a, 4c, 5a, 6a, 7b, 8c, 9c, 10a, 11c

There's room to move on the beach at the Mar Menor

❼ What does the Arabic prefix "beni" signify in many Spanish place names?
a) Son of ...
b) Father of ...
c) Uncle of ...

❽ Which national hero first conquered the city of València in 1094?
a) Don Quijote
b) Sancho Panza
c) El Cid

❾ What is burned at *Las Fallas* in València?
a) Paella
b) Big piles of wood
c) Figures made from papier-mâché

❿ Which regional landmark was designed by architect Santiago Calatrava?
a) The City of Arts and Sciences in València
b) The Casa Carbonell in Alicante
c) The 47-storey high-rise Intempo in Benidorm

⓫ What does the Valencian word *avinguda* mean in English?
a) Bon appetit!
b) Welcome!
c) Wide street or avenue

INDEX

WE WANT TO HEAR FROM YOU!

Did you have a great holiday? Is there something on your mind? Whatever it is, let us know! Whether you want to praise the guide, alert us to errors or give us a personal tip – MARCO POLO would be pleased to hear from you.
Please contact us by email:

sales@heartwoodpublishing.co.uk

We do everything we can to provide the very latest information for your trip. Nevertheless, despite all of our authors' thorough research, errors can creep in. MARCO POLO does not accept any liability for this.

PICTURE CREDITS
Cover photo: Playa de La Caleta near Villajoyosa (La Vila Joiosa) (Schapowalow: R. Schmid)
Photos: Glenkar/Shutterstock.com (6/7) Getty Images/Imgorthand (12); Getty Images/Lonely Planet Images: A. Maiquez (37); R. M. Gill (104/105, 112/113); huber-images: F. Carovillano (86), Gräfenhain (95), T. Richard (8/9, 30), R. Schmid (front outside flap, front inside flap/1, 74, 89, 130/131), R. Taylor (85), H. Williamson (90); D. Izquierdo (50); Laif: M.-O. Schulz (66); Laif/VWPicsRedux: L. Vallecillos (61); Look/age fotostock (2/3, 16/17, 54/55, 56/57, 78); mauritius images/age/Facto Foto (back inside flap); mauritius images/age/SCFoto: S. Crump (107); mauritius images/Alamy: E. Linssen (65), A. Paredes (132/133), J. Wlodarczyk (80/81); mauritius images/Foodanddrinkphotos: D. Wood (28/29); mauritius images/Hemis.fr: R. Mattes (6/7); mauritius images/Imagebroker (21, 22); mauritius images/imageBRO-KER: B. Boensch (62); mauritius images/Pixtal (26/27); mauritius-images/age fotostock: G. Azumendi (68/69), J. Peral (120/121), H. Wetzer (25); mauritius-images/Alamy: S. Abraham (82), J. Bautista (53), H. Corneli (34/35), C. Henriksen (108/109), A. Segre (32/33), A. Tihonovs (77), Tomka (48), J. Tutor (45); mauritius-images/Alamy/Freeartist (40/41); mauritius-images/Alamy/Seahotoart (102); mauritius-images/Alamy/SOPA Images Limited (33 r.); mauritius-images/hemis. fr: B. Gardel (11); mauritius-images/imageBroker: S. Kiefer (29 r.), M. Riedo (46), F. von Poser (123); Okapia/imageBROKER: F. v. Poser (93); picture alliance/Arco Images: B. Boensch (98/99); picture alliance/Shotshop/Monkey Business (13); Schapowalow/4Corners: R. Taylor (70/71); Schapow-alow/SIME: A. Saffo (14/15); Shutterstock.com: Glenkar (6/7), Marc Venema (33); vario images/imageBROKER (10, 97); F. von Poser (135); T. P. Widmann (111)

4th Edition – fully revised and updated 2023
Worldwide Distribution: Heartwood Publishing Ltd, Bath, United Kingdom
www.heartwoodpublishing.co.uk

Authors: Andreas Drouve, Fabian von Poser
Editor: Jochen Schürmann
Picture editor: Gabriele Forst
Cartography: © MAIRDUMONT, Ostfildern (pp. 38–39, 114, 117, 119, outside jacket, pull-out map; © MAIRDUMONT, Ostfildern, using data from OpenStreetMap, licence CC-BY-SA 2.0 (pp. 42–43, 58–59, 72–73, 100–101)
Cover design and pull-out map cover design: bilekjaeger_Kreativagentur with Zukunftswerkstatt, Stuttgart
Page design: Langenstein Communication GmbH, Ludwigsburg

Heartwood Publishing credits:
Translated from the German by Madeleine Taylor-Laidler, Robert Scott McInnes and Lindsay Chalmers-Gerbracht
Editors: Felicity Laughton, Kate Michell, Sophie Blacksell Jones
Prepress: Summerlane Books, Bath
Printed in India

MARCO POLO AUTHOR
FABIAN VON POSER

Fabian von Poser was born in Hamburg, Germany, in 1969 and first visited the Costa Blanca before he was even born! His parents bought a finca near Altea back in 1965, and he has travelled up and down Spain's south-east coast his whole life. Fabian's writing has featured in a range of German and international journals and magazines over the past 25 years *(fabianvonposer.com)*.

DOS & DON'TS

HOW TO AVOID SLIP-UPS & BLUNDERS

DON'T JOIN A HALF-EMPTY TABLE

If you see some free chairs at a table in a busy restaurant or café, you might feel like asking the people sitting there if they mind you joining them. But don't! This practice is completely unknown in Spain, although sitting down at the bar is fine.

DO SAVE WATER

Tourists flock to the Costa Blanca for its dry climate, but sparse rainfall, millions of swimming pools, and water and amusement parks have fuelled extreme water shortages. That's why it's important to save water wherever possible – showering, bathing, washing, in the kitchen – wherever!

DON'T DRINK & DRIVE

In Spain, the drink-drive limits are 0.5g of alcohol per ml in the blood and 0.25g per ml for breath tests. There are frequent road traffic accidents, especially on busy coastal roads such as the N-332 between Cartagena and València. Don't risk it!

DON'T START A FIRE

Helicopters and firefighting planes are a common sound from June until well into the autumn: the Costa Blanca has a fire problem. The drought, especially south of València, increases the risk of accidentally starting a forest fire. That means: don't throw away any cigarette butts, don't light any fires and be careful even when barbecuing in the garden!